WHAT'S THE POINT OF MEN'S MINISTRY?

VAL FRASER

Published by inhousemedia

Copyright © Val Fraser 2019

The right of Val Fraser to be identified as the Author of the Work has been asserted by her in accordance with the Copyright, Designs and Patents Act 1988.

All rights reserved. No part of this publication may be reproduced, stored in a retrieval system, in any form or by any means whatsoever without the prior written permission of the publishers, nor be otherwise circulated in any form of binding or cover other than that in which it is published and without a similar condition being imposed on the subsequent purchaser. Brief quotations may be embedded in critical articles or reviews.

ISBN: 978-0-9935749-5-5

Every reasonable effort has been made to trace copyright holders of material in this book, but if any have been inadvertently overlooked the publishers would be glad to hear from them and insert appropriate acknowledgements in any subsequent printing of this publication.

CONTENTS

1: CLIMATE CHANGE 5
2: WORDS 15
3: WE WAS ROBBED 25
4: MRS UNWIN 37
5: TOP JOB 49
6: DIVISION 61
7: POO 73
8: A TISSUE 85
9: STATINS 97
10: ARENA 109
11: RESPONDENTS 121

ACKNOWLEDGEMENTS

Throughout this book names and identities have been changed to protect privacy. Thank you to each person who agreed to share their story, without you this book would not be possible.

I: CLIMATE CHANGE

Over ten years ago I found myself standing on the side lines of the UK men's ministry scene. It was as if I just sort of casually noticed it one sunny morning. Like a spindly young tree growing wild, near a stream, in the farmer's field just beyond the garden boundary. I wasn't precisely sure when it had taken root and begun growing up through the undergrowth. But there it was. A new life. Just visible above the fence line. Taller, well established trees overshadowed the weedy sapling. And as I pegged the washing out with some degree of satisfaction for the first time that spring, I wondered whether the little tree would survive the summer, or even whether the farmer wanted it growing on his patch in the first place.

I watched the wild young tree, along with the UK men's ministry movement, emerging slowly, almost un-noticed at first. From a safe distance I observed them both guzzling up whatever rain and sun they could grab hold of. Tender new leaves began sprouting here and there. From within the walls of my own chaotic life I peered through my window of indifference and I saw them both bend violently under the power of the whippy wind. I watched them endure snow and frost and scorching sun and die and resurrect in season.

The big noise of a working chain saw or the distant chop-chop of a pair of shears would draw my eyes curiously towards the tree, and I would note its continued survival. The big voices of objection and the silent up-turned-noses of disapproval would draw my eyes curiously towards the men's movement, and I would note its continued survival also.

So the sun shone, and the rain fell, and the wind whipped, and the chainsaw sawed, and shears chopped, and the tree grew.

But these were not my stories. I had no part or power in how they might unfold. I had little interest, zero involvement and zero influence. This was not my tree. This was not my patch. This was not my ministry. This was not my concern.

About that time I also noticed an emerging media narrative. A strong, vocal, mostly female, commentary. These voices played out in the media and in literature. Sometimes the narrative was balanced and accurate and I felt comfortable and enlightened upon hearing it. Stories which reported and celebrated the significant achievements of women in both the past and the present were inspirational and encouraging. At other times the narrative seemed unbalanced, negative, bitter and unkind. Some narratives which lifted women up did so partially at the expense of putting men down.

During that same period I was responsible for running a Communications Department which encompassed both marketing and PR. As part of my job I became very familiar with current and emerging channels of communication. The rise of digital communications was revolutionary. It heralded a new age in news distribution. The internet became more established, with websites and e-newsletters growing in popularity. Traditional print industries, including newspapers, struggled to compete and their unrivalled position of influence began to fade. The last decade has seen a massive shift in how we receive information, be that news or opinion. With the advance of social media anyone who has a smart phone, has a voice. Everyone can tell their story, share their views, or peddle their agenda directly to the public.

Like many change activists, women have optimised the ever shifting platforms of social media to tell their stories and voice their opinions. For some this is a liberating, cathartic experience which draws attention to many wrongs, in the hopes of putting them right. Worthy causes and new business ventures have achieved platform and position, right alongside everyone else. At face value social media has created a level playing field upon which the unedited, uncompromised, unhindered voices of women can be heard just as clearly as the men's voices.

However there is considerable evidence to suggest that women are more relational and conversational than men. I notice that my female friends spend more time on social media. They have more to say than their male counterparts, post more frequently and use their platforms more efficiently. In some Facebook groups I belong to, I've observed that women's comments outnumber men's comments by two to one. When a contentious issue arises, the women pile in with considerable vigour. Robustly stating their arguments and frequently getting the last word in. I'm generalising of course, but in a world where words matter, women are very good at navigating the conversational world of social media and making their views known, leaving some of the men, and their messages, far behind.

While social media is a powerful tool for communication and many have utilised it for great good there is also a dark side. Along with the uprising of social media there has been an uprising of naysayers, commonly known as haters and trolls. As part of my working life I've had some responsibility for managing and monitoring digital media accounts on behalf of others. It has greatly saddened me to witness the distasteful efforts some of these troubled 'haters' make to gain attention for themselves. Another unpleasant aspect of social media is what some refer to as a culture of outrage. Seemingly harmless comments can engender the cruellest of tirades and 'virtue signalling'. Before you know it others have piled in to vent their own outrage from a safe distance and a comment has gone 'viral'.

> WHILE SOCIAL MEDIA IS A POWERFUL TOOL FOR COMMUNICATION AND MANY HAVE UTILISED IT FOR GREAT GOOD THERE IS ALSO A DARK SIDE.

And as if a culture of outrage weren't enough, along with the trolls and haters, we also have the fakers. It was with considerable smugness one morning that I announced gleefully to my husband that the very handsome, famous and wealthy country music legend, Kenny Rogers, had taken great interest in me. He began following me on Twitter and had sent me a private message, affectionately addressing me as 'my darling'. Soon thereafter yet another equally amorous Kenny Rogers began following me. With just a handful of followers between them it was obvious that neither of them was in fact the real live Kenny Rogers. Shortly thereafter I was followed by Davina McCall, Amanda Holden, His Royal Highness Prince Harry, Her Royal Highness the Queen, several highly decorated military men, God, Jesus, and then finally, the Prince of Darkness, Satan himself. In my estimation the authenticity of these imaginative online identities is somewhat questionable :)

In recent times stories surrounding gender rights, gender roles, gender equality, gender transformation, gender fluidity and gender identity regularly make the headlines. The existence of absolute male-ness and female-ness is being questioned. There is confusion, uncertainty, genuine nervousness and a fair bit of tip-toeing around when it comes to issues surrounding gender. The waters have become muddy.

In the last ten years there has been a rise in powerful social media platforms where keyboard warriors play out their war of words, battle lines are drawn and public opinion is shaped. Many previously unheard female voices publish their stories on these platforms as a popular media narrative. However healthy or unhealthy, however positive or negative, however balanced or unbalanced, however gracious or ungracious, the messages are having an impact.

Whether we acknowledge it or not we are currently living in a climate of thriving vocality, difficult questions, female unrest and even sinister outrage. It is under the intense pressure of these cultural conditions that the UK men's ministry movement has emerged.

My Story: A parallel process

At 3:00am one midsummer's night I was woken up by the alarming sounds of a frightened horse in some considerable distress. The noise was truly terrible. The horse seemed to be stamping and kicking the stable walls frantically and making awful crying sounds. I had never heard anything like it before and leaped to the window suspecting some kind of foul play. Two days later a baby foal trotted cautiously into the field with its mother. The foal was a stunning creature. Its rich amber coat contrasted dramatically with a flowing golden mane and tail. Within days it was crashing round the field, crashing round the tree. It was admired by all, bursting with life, a beautiful, bouncy, untamed thing.

One late autumn afternoon I noticed a strong, musty smell wafting in from the farmer's field. A huge swathe of Himalayan Balsam had invaded the field, colonising the entire perimeter. The pink flowers were swaying in the wind, spreading their sickly scent far and wide. The dense canopy was stealing light from the smaller, native wild flowers which usually thrived.

On boxing day morning, bleary eyed from Christmas festivities, I looked out of a bedroom window to see the trees reflected in the road below. In the road? I blinked. Flood waters had covered the tarmac. At the rear of the house the farmer's field had completely disappeared under a lake.

So the sun shone, and the rain fell, and the wind whipped, and the chainsaw sawed, and the shears chopped, and the foal crashed about, and the Himalayan Balsam invaded, and the flood waters rose, and still the tree grew.

But these were not my stories. I had no part or power in how they might unfold. I had zero involvement and zero influence. This was not my tree. This was not my patch. This was not my ministry. This was not my concern.

> BUT THESE WERE NOT MY STORIES. I HAD NO PART OR POWER IN HOW THEY MIGHT UNFOLD. I HAD ZERO INVOLVEMENT AND ZERO INFLUENCE. THIS WAS NOT MY TREE. THIS WAS NOT MY PATCH. THIS WAS NOT MY MINISTRY. THIS WAS NOT MY CONCERN.

QUESTIONS FOR SMALL GROUP DISCUSSION

WHICH SOCIAL MEDIA PLATFORMS DO YOU ENGAGE WITH AND WHY?

HOW FREQUENTLY DO YOU ENGAGE ON SOCIAL MEDIA?

WHAT INSPIRES YOU THE MOST ON SOCIAL MEDIA?

WHAT TROUBLES YOU THE MOST ON SOCIAL MEDIA?

WHAT IS YOUR VIEW OF TAKING A 'FAST' FROM SOCIAL MEDIA?

2: WORDS

When one people group, regardless of who they are, builds themselves up at the expense of putting another people group down, I feel uncomfortable on two counts:

I: SHORTCUTS

Our minds are naturally inclined to take a shortcut by grouping people together in one lump. This approach makes if faster and easier to make sense of the world in which we live and aids our chances of survival. We are able to bypass the lengthy operation of processing vast amounts of information. We simply inhale the salient points, quickly meld them with our existing knowledge, and arrive at a super fast conclusion. I reckon this mental shorthand is activated to protect us from threats to our existence, safety and well-being. It's a great survival skill to have. But we must be aware when it's operating and manage it wisely. Most of the time, in the civilised west, it must operate as the servant and not the master, and we need to evaluate each new situation we are faced with.

For example, when a herd of cows came charging towards me while out on a country walk, I chose to heed the shorthand signal, mentally lumping the cows together as one threatening group and running for the exit gate in fear for my life. But lumping people or cows together into one group or unit is not without cost, as it runs the risk of diminishing their value and unique identity as individuals. It may serve our purposes well in the heat of the moment, but it can be massively unfair to both individual cows and individual people who are on the receiving end of our shallow judgements.

For all I know Daisy the cow, in spite of her threatening appearance and considerable size, may be a gentle old girl who supplies copious amounts of delicious milk for the farmer, is a wonderful mother to her calves and has absolutely no intention of trampling me to death.

While we, on the other hand, may self-identify with a particular 'tribe' or people group it doesn't necessarily follow that from that point onwards we will all operate under a collective consciousness. There may be some shared thinking and some shared values but we remain as individuals who are responsible for our own actions. Is it wiser and kinder therefore, in the absence of a real threat, to assess matters case by case, as far as possible without bias or prejudice, based on individual character and merit?

Here is a case in point: Time and time again I've heard angry, wounded, women spit out, then pass on, that popular female assertion of: "All men are ba****ds". Though there may be some evidence to substantiate this claim, unless and until one has actually met every man on the planet, or at least conducted a comprehensive survey, one cannot honestly make this claim. What this voice might actually be saying is: "All the men who I've encountered up to this point in my life are, in my personal opinion, ba****ds."

If all the men which this speaker has yet to meet are treated as being guilty until proven innocent, wouldn't their statement have the potential to become a self-fulfilling prophecy? Surely if you treat someone with contempt and caution because you already believe them to be a ba****d they may well opt out of the interaction and distance themselves from you. And surely if that is the true and accurate experience of many women wouldn't they welcome a movement whose stated aims are to reverse that position?

2: ALL ARE EQUAL

So in Christ Jesus you are all children of God through faith, for all of you who were baptised into Christ have clothed yourselves with Christ. There is neither Jew nor Gentile, neither slave nor free, nor is there male and female, for you are all one in Christ Jesus. If you belong to Christ, then you are Abraham's seed, and heirs according to the promise. Galatians 3:26-29 NIV.

If I'm understanding this correctly, the apostle Paul is making an astonishing statement. He appears to be asserting the equality of men and women. How do you see this verse? How does this verse affect the way you interact with others?

As recently as 2018 I attended a women only Christian meeting at which a male church leader was invited to make a short introductory address. And the irony of that last statement is not lost on me. As he stood up from the main seating area and approached the microphone on the platform there was considerable chatter in the room as the women settled down into their seats following a social time which included a meal. He took the microphone in his hand and sternly shouted:

"Silence ladies! There's a man speaking now!"

He was deadly serious. And totally convinced of his authority over us. And no one challenged him! In

2018? In the UK? A man is allowed to address a women's meeting in that way? Seriously? All of the women in the room instantly shut up. Including myself. But I'm afraid my silence was caused more by shock and disbelief than by obedience to this windbag! I found out later that some of us were privately cheesed off about it. And moments like that don't happen in isolation, they accrue.

> SOME WOMEN ARE TIRED OF BEING PATRONISED. AND MAYBE THAT ANGER IS FUELLING SOME OF THE UNBALANCED NEGATIVE MEDIA NARRATIVE. AND THAT IN TURN FOSTERS DISTRUST, DISUNITY AND DIVISION BETWEEN MEN AND WOMEN.

So some women, both inside and outside the walls of church, are now demonstrating a knee-jerk reaction to this sort of control from men. Some women are tired of being patronised. And maybe that anger is fuelling some of the unbalanced negative media narrative. And that in turn fosters distrust, disunity and division between men and women. They become encamped on opposite sides, the battle lines are drawn, and desperate attempts are made to take back ground from each other. So nobody wins. And surely that can't be an ok thing, can it?

Sometimes, particularly on social media, people use their own words as weapons to squash the point someone else is making. At other times I notice they employ the words of others to shore up their own position.

How many times have you heard comments which open with the expression "they say"? In Christian circles it is very common to hear the term "the Bible says". It's also become popular to open arguments and counter arguments using the following terms "the media says", "science says" and even "the internet says". Accrediting statements using these vague terms all seems a bit wishy-washy to me and I'm left asking: "who exactly made that claim/declaration?" When their identity is established then my next move would be to look at their experience and credentials. I would do that to inform my own critical thinking.

My position may seem harsh but here it is: I don't take career advice from the long term unemployed, I don't take relationship advice from the long term friendless and I don't take health advice from the long term unhealthy. In the fast moving world of social media, it's worth pausing to consider exactly who is issuing the statement we are about to imbibe.

Another thing to take into consideration is intention. While only God can see the heart, it's worth pausing and praying before reacting or posting. It's worth asking:

What is the intention of this person?

Are they speaking from a position of knowledge or ignorance?

Is it there intention to just blow off steam (however wise/unwise that may be)?

Several times a week I notice that someone is posting negative or critical comments on one or other of the social media platforms which I frequent. Often these negative comments are pointing out someone else's negative behaviour. This can stir up a feeling of obligation to point out how negative they are being about someone else's negativity! But with the grace of God I refrain from commenting because I don't want to add further fuel to the growing mountain of negativity. I reckon there are enough critics in the world, and I want to be an encourager.

> I RECKON THERE ARE ENOUGH CRITICS IN THE WORLD, AND I WANT TO BE AN ENCOURAGER.

Questions for Small Group Discussion

Which animal do you fear the most? On what grounds?

Have you ever given someone the benefit of the doubt?

How important is it to consider intentions?

Have you ever made a comment which you regretted later?

3: WE WAS ROBBED

"And boys" barked Mrs Unwin, summoning up her deathliest death stare, "don't shout!"

Mrs Howard's fingers dutifully plonked out the familiar notes of the first line before turning to face the eager assembly with a definitive, conductor like nod. And then we were away. Boys, girls and teachers alike. All singing in triumphant unison. Not shouting. We were singing. Our combined voices soared upwards to kiss the ancient oak rafters, before swirling and falling back down to the herringbone floor only to execute a resounding bounce back upwards. The vast wall of sound filled the old school hall to bursting. Its energy and life were unstoppable, permeating every deep red brick, soaking every crafted bone of wood, crashing out through every fragile pane of brittle glass. The sound of our voices plunged into the majestic open fireplace before ascending upwards and escaping up through the towering twisted chimney stacks into the waiting arms of heaven.

And surely happy little hearts were touched, softened, moulded and shaped in the refining crucible of praise. Certainly mine was. Such is the transforming power of worship. Even a child, or dare I say, especially a child, whose heart is yet uncluttered by the cares of adult life, can experience the mystery of divine connection during such enthralling moments of corporate abandonment.

But what of those hearts which had been previously scolded? What of the hearts which were oppressed by the preceding threat? What of the voices which were holding back their shouts? Struggling to contain themselves?

What about the boys?

Boys who would one day become men, boys who must learn that they may not release the full expression of their voices and emotions before God.

Or perhaps anyone. Boys who learned that holding back is an essential requirement of polite society. That maybe God is an angry task master, in the shape of a glaring, bossy, controlling madam who heartily disapproves of shouting and energy and enthusiasm and excitement and noise and expression and joyful abandonment.

Even when channelled with fervent gusto into a favourite traditional hymn. Even when it is that most rousing of battle cries which we know and love as 'Onward Christian Soldiers'? Even then? Even in a gathering of Christians for the express purpose of worship, raised voices are forbidden and scorned and frowned upon?

Really?

Why? Why must they not shout?

Why?! Why?! Why?!

I longed to ask. As a child 'why' was the word which burned most strongly within me (no change there then). What possible harm could shouting do? Was shouting harmful? To the voice? To the ear drums? To the lungs? Would someone hyper ventilate and pass out? Or vomit? Who would hear the shouting? Who would object? Wasn't the entire population of the school right here in the assembly? Surely this particular hymn was written for exactly such boys, boys who needed to channel their considerable young energy into something positive. Why not channel it into this? Into singing? Into praising? Why not blow off some steam? I didn't get it. I didn't get it then, and I don't get it now.

I may never know exactly why Mrs Unwin disapproved of boys shouting during 'Onward Christian Soldiers'. However, in my more gracious moments I have wondered whether the idea of soldiers 'marching as to war' touched a nerve in her?

The ability to calculate someone's age, and subsequently their place in history, is a mysterious process for the very young. All adults appear equally ancient to children because they lack the perspective needed to untangle the degrees of age. However, I have retrospectively calculated Mrs Unwin's date of birth, her precise age during my own school years, and therefore her exact place in British history. My calculations are based upon my sketchy recollection of the towering frothy hat which she wore for the annual church procession or 'walking day' as we called it back then. And while I readily concede that hats are by no means a reliable indicator of age, that is my only frame of reference and thus, I have implemented it to good use.

By my current reckoning Mrs Unwin would have been a young girl during World War Two. Even if she herself did not lose a loved one, she almost certainly would have known someone who did. No one living during those dreadful war years could have escaped the effects and impact of war.

Yet even in the light of these new, kinder thoughts, which give her the benefit of the doubt, I remain confused as to her thinking. If her aim was to discourage these impressionable young boys in her care from being stirred up by the culturally unacceptable, aggressive, unpopular, language of war, rather than to discourage them from the act of worship, why choose that hymn in the first place? There were tons of other hymns in the book! Did she think that shouting would over excite the boys? That it would cause an uncontrollable brawl to break out? Or was she somewhat less than the pillar of society I perceived her to be, and had simply arrived at work that morning nursing a raging hangover?

> THOSE BOYS WERE ROBBED. THE BOYS I WENT TO SCHOOL WITH, WHO ARE NOW GROWN MEN (EACH WITH THEIR OWN PARTICULAR INFLUENCE ON OUR WORLD FOR GOOD OR ILL), WERE ROBBED OF SINGING THEIR FAVOURITE HYMN WITH ALL THEIR HEARTS. BUT MUCH MORE IMPORTANTLY, THEY WERE ROBBED OF THE TRANSFORMATIONAL POWER OF WORSHIP.

I will never know her true reasons. But this I do know. They were robbed. Those boys were robbed. The boys I went to school with, who are now grown men (each with their own particular influence on our world for good or ill), were robbed of singing their favourite hymn with all their hearts. But much more importantly, they were robbed of the transformational power of worship. And who knows what damage that has done? What changes in their hearts might have occurred during that mysterious spiritual transaction which Christians sometimes refer to as 'deep calling to deep'?

What different sort of men might they have become should they have encountered the divine that day, and the many other, similar days? Yes, some of them might have been shouting for shouting's sake, showing off to their mates. But I believe that some might have been reaching out to their Heavenly Father. There may have been a genuine calling upwards to their Creator, an authentic searching for that divine connection which can wake up the best in us and transform a life. In each of those young boys there may well have been the beginnings of an open-ness, an offering and a receiving from Him.

Just as there was for me. An obedient little girl. A child who was neither scolded, nor instructed to hold back. I was given the priceless gift of absolute freedom in worshipping, fully from the heart, I was given access to the transformational power of worship. A power which has been at work in me ever since that time. And furthermore I was gladly accepted, just as I am, and granted free, unhindered, 'access all areas' membership, joining with that eternal company of worshipers both on earth and in heaven. The magnitude of those three words "boys, don't shout" troubles me to this day, many years after the event.

I have it on very good authority that singing in prison, at the top of your voice, in the middle of the night, is extremely dangerous for your health. It's an activity which even the most hardened criminals dare not undertake. Not only could it put you at risk of severe and repeated beatings from your fellow inmates, it could make you a vulnerable outcast who is subjected to a myriad of daily, unthinkable cruelties. Even the prison guards may withdraw what little measure of compassion and protection they may have previously afforded you. But this is exactly what Paul and Silas did while they were incarcerated in a brutal prison, the Alcatraz of their day. They were locked up in an institution with zero human rights, zero food, and a reliance on outside help to supply even their basic needs. If ever two boys needed Mrs Unwin to instruct them to shut up and calm down, it was Paul and Silas.

But Paul and Silas didn't shut up and calm down. They let rip! They were off their heads on worshipping, singing and praising God, placing themselves, might I suggest, under even greater risk than they were already experiencing. And yet, their non-worshipping inmates, probably all male, probably all criminals, probably all equally desperate, were not scolding or threatening them at all. According to the short written account of this event, in Acts 16:25, they were listening. They were held in silence under the mantle of praise, surely something was happening to them.

Were the ears of their spirits being opened? Was God at work in them also? Is this why they weren't objecting, but remained silent, listening to the praise, taking it in? Does honest audible worship have the power to reach right into the hardened heart of a non-believing man? Does God use the praises of His people to bypass the mind and connect with souls?

And when the praises of Paul and Silas were in full flow, God caused an earthquake which broke their physical chains and flung open the prison doors! These two worshippers became free from their captivity, and remarkably, the apparently non-worshipping captives were likewise released. The story of Paul and Silas very clearly demonstrates that authentic, audible, sung worship is an extremely powerful tool which God uses to release the hearts of captive men (and women). The freedom is made available to both the worshiper and those hearing the worship. If worship is so powerful why do I see so many effective campaigns to neutralise it, stifle it, shut it down, limit it, put the brakes on it, calm it down, shut it up, nip it in the bud, control it, put a lid on it, don't let it get out of hand? Subtle campaigns which effectively discriminate against men with a hidden message ordering: "boys, don't shout!"

In spite of the many incidents of gross unfairness, disadvantage, sexual harassment, abuse and exploitation which I have experienced on account of being female, in all fairness, this was not one of those occasions. Not at all. I believe that, in that particular setting, on that particular day it was the boys in the group who were placed at a disadvantage, somewhat dis-empowered, slighted, squashed, suppressed, controlled. In that setting the little girls had the upper hand because all we had to do was be ourselves. And I have to ask myself, was this in part because, during that season, there was a woman directing operations? Ok, so it was a modest operation, no more than a group of very young children singing in an English urban village school. But she was most definitely calling the shots. (Can you imagine the head teacher of a Welsh village school taking any stance which would suppress the splendour and volume of the masculine voice?)

Setting aside the spiritual dimension in this dynamic, how might the boys in question have been affected, purely in their natural selves? What message did this stern, anticipatory telling off, send to their young minds? I'm left wondering if they, as grown men, remember the occasion and how it has affected their view of expressing themselves. I imagine half of them to be timid, 'cowed' and expert in the manipulations of passive aggressive behaviour. The other half to be seen regularly shouting their lungs out at sporting events or outside the pub late on Friday night. I wonder how many went on to develop an appreciation of singing, of music, of worship, or of the divine?

Questions for Small Group Discussion

Did you grow up around girls?

Did you grow up around boys?

What is your earliest memory of worship?

Have you experienced God's presence during worship?

Have you ever been inside a prison?

What is your favourite worship song?

4: MRS UNWIN

Speaking figuratively, why are there so many Mrs Unwins? Why are there so many hurdles which get in the way of men freely worshipping? The high un-singable tunes. The flouncy lyrics. The constant calls to stand-up-sit-down. The bitty stop-start programmes.

Dare I suggest the unfashionable possibility that men and women might be different? Dare I suggest that some men and some women may even sit at opposite ends of a continuum, or at different points along a continuum? Not just physically but spiritually?

Following a particularly excitable women only worship event a deeply religious female friend approached me unbidden, and breathlessly revealed, with some satisfaction: "Women are just so much more spiritual than men, aren't they?" I was completely taken aback by this private assertion and just smiled weakly, in a kind of neutral, wishy-washy abstention.

What I had witnessed at the meeting was certainly worship, yes indeed! But also a lot of raw, unedited emotions. There were copious amounts of tears, snot, laughter, embracing, singing, prophetic words, expressive hand waving and even dance. I heard much psychological stroking along with soothing, kind words. There were cathartic conversations, confessions and crying. There were affirming declarations from scripture about love, identity and belonging. There were many open, gushing, sincere, heartfelt declarations of love for the Lord. The majority of these declarations employed the kind of flattering, sugary sweet language we might enjoy hearing from a romantic partner. Someone who had in the heat of that very moment, just discovered that they had fallen deeply in love with us, and we were the most wonderful creature on the planet. There was considerable evidence that evening to support the claim that women are more emotional than men, but I'm not clear how we might measure and compare their degree of spirituality.

Putting aside any cynical accusations of projection or exhibitionism, I truly believe these ladies were sincere and earnest in their sentiments, their deep friendship with each other, their worship, and their absolute dedication to Christ. To use popular yet direct language, it was all a bit 'girly'. And personally, as a girly girl myself, I don't actually have any problem with that. Most of the time. This was a fairly private meeting, and in many ways it was a perfectly safe place in which to express and release strong emotions wholly unabated. The female equivalent, if you will, of stadium sports.

I know from personal experience that expressive worship in some churches makes many folks feel uncomfortable. Even the perfectly reasonable act of shedding a few tears while remembering my late Father during 'The Father's Love' in church on Fathers' Day generated an email from someone enquiring about my mental health. But at the Ladies only meeting there was no such concern, just acceptance and deep sisterly love. It was great! But I understand how some might struggle to engage with the unstructured wildness of that emotionally charged atmosphere, whatever their gender.

One beautifully feminine, caring friend, who describes herself as 'methodical' is a case in point. Her firm verdict on all this gushing? Giving me some serious side eyes, she asserted: "There's no need for it, Val, there's just no need for it."

So what might we surmise are some of the differences between men and women in regard to worship?

Allow me first to clarify what kind of worship I'm referring to here. While I accept that there are many different definitions and forms of worship, I'm speaking here of corporate, sung, audible worship. At one end of this spectrum we might find two men spontaneously singing, unaccompanied, in a prison cell at midnight. At the other end of the spectrum we might find a fully orchestrated, worship event in a building which has been opened to the public such as a Cathedral. This kind of worship may be 'led' and directed by someone, perhaps a choir, band or a worship leader. Many of us who call ourselves Christians will have found ourselves sitting in such a gathering. Often on a Sunday. Often on a very hard pew.

Before offering any further suggestions, I must first beg your forgiveness, for I am about to typecast the male and female personas. It's a lazy, thoroughly out-dated practice which I personally abhor. Around about the point in a book when male/female stereotypes appear I would most likely throw said book across the room in outrage before storming off to the kitchen to make toast and jam, as a form of mild protest. As I'm wheat intolerant that would be a spectacularly immature protest to stage. I'm the primary victim of that action and would suffer from crippling pain within a few hours. After consuming said toast I would return to pick the book up again and continue reading in the short pain-free window which remained. But now I would be armed with an unhealthy level of disdain for the author, further aggravating my delicate digestive system.

Unpacking issues around men and women is a proverbial time bomb in our gender sensitive culture. None of us wants to be typecast as anything, because we're all unique individuals, not slaves to our gender. But the reality is we do live in a physical world, with physical bodies, which can have a profound effect upon our thinking, our behaviour and our preferences. So when I refer to men and women I'm speaking here in the absolute broadest terms imaginable.

> SO WHEN I REFER TO MEN AND WOMEN I'M SPEAKING HERE IN THE ABSOLUTE BROADEST TERMS IMAGINABLE.

Let's start with hummus.

Because worship is a lot like hummus.

Some people enjoy hummus. But some people don't see the point of hummus. Some people disagree about the correct spelling of hummus/houmous. When there is hummus at a buffet some people will walk right past it and head straight for the sausage rolls, but others will dive right into the hummus. Some people like plain hummus and some prefer the low fat or spicy versions. Whichever way you look at it hummus is a lot like worship because it's high in protein and fibre which both do good things on the inside of you.

But hummus, much like worship is not always great to look at. Hummus is not a visually pleasing food. In fact if you'd never tasted hummus you could be forgiven for not wanting to try it, based on how it looks. It would be perfectly understandable to not want to give it a go in the first place. Hummus manufacturers seem to understand that, in the first instance, hummus doesn't look particularly edible to the human eye. So in order to sell their product they wrap it up in attractive, earthy, wholesome packaging to tempt the consumer. But when you get your hummus home and put a dollop on your free-from oat digestive biscuit it still looks like an ikky, beige, questionable mush.

Eating hummus is counter intuitive. The eyes hesitate over it, until the tongue remembers and tastes it again, do this enough times and you will become desensitised to just how non-edible hummus looks. You will forget that hummus is visually ugly. You will only remember that it is experientially tasty, and innocently offer it to other people as if you are giving them a fabulous hippy treat.

Some people farm and grow chick peas which are the key ingredient of hummus. Some people enjoy preparing home-made hummus from tinned chick peas. Others find it to be time consuming, fiddly, messy and have better things to do with their energy. Some people don't see the point of exerting all the effort which is needed to make home-made hummus. They prefer to buy and consume ready-made hummus. People who buy and consume ready-made hummus have little understanding of just how much hard work and effort goes into growing chick peas, and then preparing and presenting good, tasty hummus that people will choose to eat at a buffet.

Wise people at buffets may cautiously observe others consuming hummus first, and seeing their enjoyment of it, may opt to give it a go. Once they discover hummus for themselves they may be willing to select it again at the next buffet they attend. They may even decide to buy their own ready-made hummus from the supermarket to share next time they host a buffet. Some people will only eat free hummus. And some people will never try hummus at all because it just looks too weird and ugly and their brains can't identify it as proper food. And so those people will never get to eat hummus. And worship is a lot like hummus.

Moving on from hummus.

Let's look at intimacy.

Because worship is a lot like intimacy.

Some people enjoy intimacy. But some people don't see the point of intimacy.

I'm no expert, but it's my tin pot understanding that, generally speaking, men and women are programmed to respond differently when it comes to the timings surrounding sexual arousal, intimacy and subsequent satisfaction. One popular and well accepted convention is that men get turned on to the idea of physical intimacy far quicker than women do. In our sex mad culture it's not at all wise to draw too many parallels between the physical intimacy which happens through the body and the spiritual intimacy which happens through the spirit.

And so I will draw just one parallel, and that is in the area of timing. I'm suggesting that it's in this area of programmed timings where men and women differ in their encounters with the divine during sung, audible, worship. It's my observation that women are more responsive than men and need less time, and less effort, to 'warm up'. Some women will leap right into the flow of worship leaving their male counterparts far behind. By the time the men do catch up it's all over with, and they have missed the moment entirely. Perhaps, this eagerness of the female heart is what my breathless friend was getting at when she claimed that women are more spiritual than men.

Christian Vision for Men (CVM) Regional Director England (North West) Bob Fraser is perhaps better known by some in the North West as a prolific singer songwriter. He was one of the early pioneers of contemporary Christian music in the UK, recording two vinyl albums as front man with the popular 70s country rock band Canaan before going on to record twelve solo albums. In his book Beyond the Banter he writes: "Men readily sing their lungs out in a stadium, but can clam up in church. They will freely roar for their sporting hero with total abandonment, but can freeze at the invitation to sing for God. In a stadium they will wave their arms, and sway and rock shoulder to shoulder with their mates, without the slightest hint of embarrassment. But then squirm uncomfortably or stand rigid in the presence of their God, robbed of the transforming power of worship."

Fraser explains how his own thinking about worship has shifted. He writes: "These days I'm intensely aware of how men experience church and worship music. I feel my current approach is more intelligible to those with little or no history of doing church. The worship songs I use in the Men's Group I run have dynamic, strong rhythms which men can follow, they fall in a musical range which isn't too high, can be comfortably sung with gusto by the average male voice, and the lyrics don't demand the mental gymnastics required for romantic declarations of love. The acid test of an all-inclusive worship song is to observe men singing. If they dip out for a line or word, either the lyrics are too girly or the notes are too high!"

QUESTIONS FOR SMALL GROUP DISCUSSION

HOW ADVENTUROUS ARE YOU AT BUFFETS?

HAVE YOU EVER SUNG IN A STADIUM?

WHAT'S THE MOST NUMBER OF PEOPLE YOU HAVE WORSHIPPED WITH?

HOW WELL DO YOU UNDERSTAND MODERN GENDER ISSUES?

HAVE YOU EVER PRAISED GOD WHILE ALONE?

5: TROUBLE AT THE TOP

Let's take a look at some of the common concerns, challenges and tensions which can arise between **busy church leaders**, men in church and the ongoing work of men's ministry.

> I NEED THE MEN IN THIS CHURCH TO GET ON WITH CLEARING ALL THOSE BRAMBLES. IT'S A MASSIVE JOB AND I CAN'T BE EXPECTED TO DO IT ALL BY MYSELF, NOW CAN I?

> AFTER THE SERVICE CAN YOU GATHER ALL THE MEN FROM YOUR GROUP TO PUT THE CHRISTMAS TREE UP, AND THE TINSEL? PLEASE? OH AND THE ANGELS TOO? AND CAN YOU PUT THE TWINKLY LIGHTS ON AS WELL?

> WE NEED THE MEN TO FORM A WORKING PARTY TO PAINT THE COMMUNITY ROOM OVER THE WEEKEND.

" ALL THESE YOUNG PEOPLE NEED MENTORING BY MATURE MEN OF FAITH. THAT'S THE MOST URGENT TASK FOR MEN, BECAUSE THESE YOUNG PEOPLE ARE THE FUTURE OF OUR CHURCH.

" THE SPINSTER OF OUR PARISH NEEDS HELP MOVING HOUSE OVER THE WEEKEND, YOU GUYS CAN DO THAT RIGHT?

" THE WIDOW IN OUR CONGREGATION NEEDS SOMEONE TO CLIMB INTO HER LOFT SPACE AND GET HER SUITCASE DOWN. YOU'RE OK WITH LADDERS RIGHT?

Every church building has an endless list of maintenance jobs. Every community of faith has an endless list of practical tasks to assist the needy. This is an area where the handy, helpful man of faith can find his fit. If he has a basic skill set and a tool box, he can succeed, indeed, he can excel! But in addition to his personal commitments and responsibilities, if he doesn't watch out, the expectations placed upon him can quickly mushroom into an overwhelming pressure. He can become discouraged when every conversation opens with the same question: "Oh, I've been looking for you, could you just . . ."

I interviewed one man who confided: "I'm so tired of being viewed as a human resource in this church and constantly being recruited to do jobs! I want to serve, but I need fellowship and pastoral care too, I'm more than just a resource!"

Another practical, willing soul who I interviewed recently shared with me: "She treats me worse than an unpaid slave! As though she has a right to my time at the weekend just because we go to the same church! The moment I complete one job for her she has the next one all lined up!"

One of the busiest, jolliest men I have ever known, the most agreeable, servant hearted soul you could ever wish to meet, privately struggles with the demands which church leaders and members inadvertently place upon him on a daily basis. He receives a constant stream of phone calls, regular knocks on his front door at odd times of the day, along with many face to face encounters when he is out and about. This guy, like many stalwarts of the church, puts in hours and hours of his own time voluntarily. The never ending requests for help overwhelm him. Some days they crush his spirit to a point where he cannot actually function. He tells me that sometimes he wants to run away from it all. He said: "Time spent in the company of Christian brothers, who demand absolutely nothing from me but fellowship, has a powerful restorative effect. It's the highlight of my month."

It's fool hardy to believe that men are happy to get on with practical tasks and need little thanks or recognition in return. During the process of interviewing many men while researching this book what I've learned is this: Men want to feel valued just as much as women do, perhaps even more so. They want to be appreciated, complimented. They want a pat on the back, they want to be included, invited, accepted. To us women men may appear to be less communicative and needy than our female friends are, but they hurt just as much as we do when they are taken for granted or have been left out. Men don't like being put upon any more than women do. One of the biggest surprises for me has been privately witnessing the sheer strength of their emotions.

In addition to this perception that the men in church should undertake responsibility for practical tasks there can be varying degrees of concern from the church leadership towards men's groups. Sometimes there is apparent support because the group brings in 'new blood'. One men's group leader shared: "Every time a particular minister attends one of our meetings he attempts to recruit help for his projects from the men who I've developed a connection with and invited. Many of them don't even go to his church."

At the other end of the spectrum is suspicion. Another men's ministry leader chuckled when he said: "My vicar openly disapproves of the men gathering together, even though I'm ordained myself, I had to agree to let the female curate join all of our meetings to keep an eye on us!"

What is it about a thriving men's group that can seem like such a threat? Should we be worried about it? Why is it that thriving women's groups, toddler groups and even youth groups don't seem to worry anyone, leaders or otherwise? What exactly is it that some church leaders get so uptight about when men gather? Is there some historical evidence that men gathering together, without women, is a bad thing for the church? Is there some clerical training that recommends caution where men's groups are concerned? Where do these fears and concerns come from? And furthermore, are they valid fears and concerns?

Could one reason be that women are (generally) more agreeable than men? According to the Youtube lectures of Canadian Professor of Clinical Psychology, Dr Jordan B Peterson, there is conclusive clinical evidence and research which says that your average woman is more agreeable than your average man. Dr Peterson seems to really know his stuff. I don't doubt his word for one moment. Think about this; many paid church leaders effectively manage a team of unpaid volunteers. The mechanics of running a church depends to a very large extent on the willingness (which could also be described as agreeableness) of volunteers to sign up for an infinite number of unpaid tasks. At my own church on any given Sunday there can be a dozen volunteers running the show and giving up their entire morning. Including preparation time ahead of the service this can add up to anything from two to ten hours of unpaid work. For someone in full time employment with limited free time that's a big sacrifice which could eat up half the weekend. Seventy per cent of the volunteers are usually female. The others are very agreeable men. Or at the very least men who have conceded to be agreeable for the duration of that morning.

And when a new church leader is appointed, agreeableness among the members is also of great benefit. Unless the new leader is simply 'cruising' until retirement, they will want to put their own stamp on the organisation. Change is absolutely inevitable. New church leaders can't implement everything by themselves, they need a team to make things happen. They need members to get behind these changes to bring them about. They need agreeable people. And if they are experienced in life they will know instinctively that woman are often more agreeable than men.

If you accept Dr Peterson's assertion (based on clinical trials) that women are generally more agreeable than men, it's not too big a leap to accept that by definition, men will generally be less agreeable than women. They may be less inclined to give up their hard earned free time to help the paid church leader. Men, especially those who feel they spend their days toiling to survive in the challenging and stressful work environment of the 'real world', may even find themselves asking the question: "what is this minister actually being paid to do?" They may consider that the church leader is getting well paid to help needy church members or to do particular tasks. Who among us sees an account of what our church leader actually does each week? Like many of us, they may have little understanding of how their church leader actually spends his time. Some folks have even voiced the opinion that the church minister has free accommodation and only works on Sundays.

Life is very difficult for many men (and women) who inhabit the brutal, competitive, cut and thrust commercial world of work outside of 'Christian Ministry'. They may privately hold the view, and publicly give off the vibe, that if the leader is being paid to do a job, they should just get on with it. This unspoken view may generate a tension in men which a savvy church leader may pick up on. The net result may be a leader who gives the guys a wide berth and prefers to hang out with the women.

One of the enormous challenges of men's ministry is the timescales. Leaders who run successful men's ministry operations make it clear that they are playing for the long game. The very long game. Men's ministry is probably unlike other ministries in that regard.

Expecting a man to make the leap from eating a couple of bacon butties with the lads on a Saturday morning to being sold out on church is a totally unrealistic outcome. The benchmark of success is not in seeing more men religiously sitting through a traditional Sunday morning service every week. Many wish it were so and bemoan the fact that it isn't. The phenomenological evidence suggests that it just doesn't work like that. The Church leader who isn't aware how slowly and cautiously men build connections can become disenchanted with men's ministry when the effort doesn't translate into bums on seats quickly enough. It's easy to conclude that there's just no point to it.

Henry (not his real name) is a lovely quiet family man with a dry sense of humour, a mature faith and a deep love of studying the word. He's attended many, many church services. He appeared to be a contented church member. But Henry was keeping a secret. He was utterly disheartened with church and had been considering giving up on it for a very long time. This was a difficult decision, but he finally decided that he was going to leave his church and never return. He shared: "I'd had enough. I was ready to give it all up and just slip away quietly without anyone noticing."

Out of the blue he received an invitation from a friend to attend a men's meeting and went along. It was at this meeting that he felt he'd received a clear word from God about 'not giving up'. Eventually Henry got involved with running the group and found new friends, new meaning and a new sense of purpose. He changed his mind about leaving and decided to stay at his church without anyone realising that he'd nearly slipped through the net.

The true effects of men's ministry can go unseen for months and years even, like roots growing beneath the soil. This is one of the factors which makes the work so challenging. Those who run men's groups really do need backup because the effort is great, the obvious rewards seem few, and it's very easy to become discouraged.

QUESTIONS FOR SMALL GROUP DISCUSSION

HAVE YOU EVER FELT UNDER-APPRECIATED BY YOUR CHURCH LEADERS?

HOW EFFECTIVE ARE YOU AT PUTTING IN PERSONAL BOUNDARIES?

IF YOU FELL INTO CRISIS TOMORROW WHO WOULD YOU CONTACT FOR SUPPORT?

HOW MANY FRIENDS WOULD FEEL ABLE TO MAKE CONTACT WITH YOU IF THEY FELL INTO A CRISIS TOMORROW?

6. DIVISION

Let's take a look at some of the common concerns, challenges and tensions which can arise between **married women**, their husbands, men in church and the ongoing work of men's ministry.

"WON'T SEPARATE MEETINGS FOR HUSBANDS AND WIVES CAUSE DIVISION IN THE LONG RUN?

"DON'T WE WANT TO ENCOURAGE COUPLES TO DEVELOP A SHARED LIFE AND A SHARED MINISTRY?

"ISN'T IT JUST SELFISH FOR MEN TO MEET UP WITH THEIR MATES ALL THE TIME? DON'T MEN NEED TO GROW UP AND TAKE RESPONSIBILITY?

" I'VE COUNSELLED SO MANY MARRIED COUPLES WHO ARE GOING THROUGH DIFFICULTIES, AND I'M TELLING YOU, THEY NEED TO SPEND MORE TIME TOGETHER, NOT LESS.

" WE HAVE ENOUGH DIVORCES IN THIS TOWN, FAMILIES NEED TO STICK TOGETHER, NOT GO OFF DOING THEIR OWN THING.

Where do your female friends stand on these issues?

How does your church leadership address these tough questions? It's not too difficult to work out. Just take a look at which ministries they get fully behind. Where do you stand? What is your response to these arguments against men's ministry?

One of the burning questions behind all these questions is this: "Do 'men only' activities build up marital relationships or do they tear them down?"

Many folks think the answer to this question is yes and yes.

Yes, men only activities have the potential to build up marital relationships.

When men's ministry is God centred, and operating at its very best, it has the potential to feed and nurture the spirit of a man. This in turn has the potential to benefit his family, his friends, his community, his boss and his team mates. When iron sharpens iron, everyone wins.

The most well attended, long running, growing men's groups in the UK offer a range of activities throughout the year. Key ingredients may include simple food, transformational worship, breakaway groups with discussions, the sharing of successes and failures, bible study, the pooling of wisdom and knowledge, peer group mentoring, prayer support, social times with fun and laughter, Father and child play mornings, exciting outdoor sports activities, uplifting conferences, rotating prayer triplets and the building of real, lasting, friendship. Though every man will not attend every event, a thriving men's ministry has the potential to offer each man the opportunity to select from a menu of wholesome, Christian based, activities. These opportunities can be liberating for the man of faith. They are particularly refreshing for the defeated, passive man of faith. And there appears to be plenty of those around.

Yes, men only activities have the potential to tear down marital relationships.

If they are unwholesome. Some men of faith will feel a high level of discomfort about taking part in what they see as the less savoury, activities the world has to offer. At face value joining the local darts team may seem like a perfectly innocent idea. But if the group culture is one of heavy drinking, smoking weed, one-up-man-ship, demeaning women, petty theft and the occasional punch up, the Christian man may face a dilemma. With the support of good friends and the grace of God he may stand his ground. Or he may seriously struggle to fit in and, for the sake of belonging to the tribe, he may compromise his principles and concede to go along with the pack mentality. Eventually he may even ditch his church connections, which may in turn put distance between himself and his wife.

Alternatively he may not feel totally comfortable spending every moment of his free time stuck at home. Television, Youtube, gardening, DIY, domestic chores, shopping, catering, childcare and the most scintillating of female conversation can only afford him so much fulfilment before 'cabin fever' and boredom sets in. After many years of this existence he may begin to die on the inside and begin longing for a little taste of adventure, excitement, even rebellion.

Many people believe that inside every man, God has placed a deep longing for fellowship, for brotherhood, for unity, for working together for a purpose. Effective, well-led men's groups can offer a sense of belonging which some men can really struggle to find within the main body of the church or the Sunday services. There is much evidence to suggest that releasing men to be part of their local men's group increases their likelihood of attending church. They are more likely to show up on a Sunday with their wives and children because their friends are there, casual follow-on conversations with other men occur more naturally and this helps them to feel like they fit in. It becomes their church, not just their wife's church.

Increasingly men are under intense pressure. Many will experience stress daily, particularly in the work place. They may work long hours with little reward and security. Perhaps the most worrying aspect of men's lives is the on-going emotional isolation they can experience. Looking at this from a female standpoint it could be argued that some of this isolation is self-imposed when a man stubbornly refuses to talk about things.

One young man told me: "95% of my existence is spent living inside my own head, sorting out my own problems, arriving at my own solutions. Most of my mates live like this as well. Perhaps it's a man thing, it's just how we're made, we don't want to open up." In addition to this "living inside my own head" thing, much of the isolation men experience is brought about by their circumstances.

In the fabulous film 'Ladies in Lavender' there are some wonderful scenes of male endeavour. It's set on the coast of Cornwall in 1936 and exudes all the innocence and charm of a bygone age. Men of all ages are seen toiling in the fields together, playing games in the pub and later celebrating a successful harvest in the village hall. For good or ill they live together in a shared community. I'd like to think that this romanticised version of men's lives is fairly representative of rural life in those days, and for centuries previously. Men didn't have to construct times when they worked shoulder to shoulder with each other, it was just a ready-made part of country life. Men had to pull together, they had to put aside their differences and get along, because bringing in a harvest, or a haul of fish, or herding livestock, or building a barn or a road, was an essential joint endeavour which ensured their continued existence.

For many centuries working together was essential for survival, while working in isolation meant danger and a potential death sentence. Perhaps there is an ancient part of our brains which senses deep down, that when we are alone, separated from the tribe, we are vulnerable and this generates a very real sense of foreboding and considerable anxiety.

For many who work in modern offices, education, media, construction, health or business, there is little or no true camaraderie in the work environment. Relationships at work seem to be more about 'networking' and 'climbing the greasy pole'. It can be a brutally harsh, dog-eat-dog environment. In a competitive environment disclosing sensitive information about rates of pay, for example, can be very unwise. An unscrupulous colleague, who wants to be promoted over you, may use any personal information as a weapon to advance their own career. During times of financial instability, when rumours of redundancies abound, the workplace can become openly hostile. It can be difficult to know who to trust or confide in. Keeping your cards close to your chest, hiding any weaknesses or failings and appearing to be succeeding in your role can seem like the best option.

Pressure to provide, perceived or otherwise, can crush a man's spirit. Spiraling debt can be a direct result of this pressure. Having no job and being stuck outside the world of work can deliver a particularly cruel brand of pain for men and women of all ages. In an average life time few men will escape the potentially emasculating blows of redundancy, unemployment, retirement and ill health; and the frightening financial consequences of those events. Many modern communities lack cohesion, people move away from their home towns, and in many places it is increasingly common for neighbours to hardly know each other at all.

The deadly combination of pressure, stress and isolation can have a profound effect on men. Most of us will know someone who has struggled with mental health problems such as depression and anxiety.

Much like church, men's groups can never be perfect, and can never precisely meet the vast and various needs of everyone who attends. And just like church, or any community or social group, they can never be a substitute for professional medical care. But they can offer a great deal of simple, preventative medicine. Good old fashioned fellowship, acceptance, friendship, prayer, conversation and laughter can go a long way towards alleviating dangerous feelings of anxiety caused by isolation and stress.

An afternoon spent walking in the hills, followed by a pub lunch with good mates who genuinely care, can put things back into perspective for many of us. Feelings of normality can return and every day burdens can seem so much lighter.

When crisis strikes, and it will at some point, the 'man down' call goes up like a flare into the night sky! And this is when the great, unfathomable Christ like power of men's ministry kicks in. These same friends, these brothers, will gather around and hold each other up. They will strengthen each other, like only men can. I've seen it happen. I've seen it work. Regular meetings offer a ready-made safety net which can afford some degree of protection for those individuals who are willing to receive it. No one needs to slip through the net. And girls, here's the real win for you: When times are hard for you and your man, this extra male support can actually take a shed load of pressure off you.

Questions for Small Group Discussion

How comfortable are you with the amount of time your romantic partner spends on individual pursuits?

How happy are you with the amount of time you spend on individual pursuits?

Some people suggest that the closeness of romantic relationships is not static but has a rhythm which ebbs and flows. How do you see it?

What economic pressures are you currently facing?

If you are part of a faith community, how would you describe your place in it?

7. POO

Let's take a look at some of the common concerns, challenges and tensions which can arise between **mums**, dads, men in church and the ongoing work of men's ministry.

" THE CHILDREN HAVE FOOTBALL, SWIMMING, DANCING AND MUSIC LESSONS. I CAN'T BE IN TWO PLACES AT ONCE. I NEED MY HUSBAND TO HELP ME WITH ALL THESE THINGS!

" MY CHILDREN WON'T BE LITTLE FOR LONG, THEIR FATHER NEEDS TO BOND WITH THEM BEFORE IT'S TOO LATE.

" THE BABY WAKES ME UP SIX OR SEVEN TIMES EVERY NIGHT. I CAN'T KEEP THIS UP. I'M ABSOLUTELY EXHAUSTED. IT'S HIS BABY TOO! MY HUSBAND NEEDS TO HELP OUT SO I CAN GRAB SOME SLEEP BEFORE I GO CRAZY!!

" I'VE SACRIFICED EVERYTHING TO PRODUCE HIS OFFSPRING! DOES HE NOT GET THAT?! IS IT TOO MUCH TO ASK THAT HE THROW A FEW LOADS OF LAUNDRY IN THE WASHER ON A SATURDAY?

There's a massive blob of bird poo on the glass roof panel of our conservatory. When the sun shines the repulsive combination of liquid and solids casts its accusing poo-shaped shadow down onto the tiled floor. You would think a pterodactyl had just flown over and bombed us. Well above my standing sight lines, there's insect poo splashed prolifically onto the inside of the glass panels. And at ceiling level, beyond my regular reach, sinister black mould is dotted along the white plastic framework. A cobweb hangs like bunting high up in one corner. And a few dead wasps are curled up in an awkward unreachable place.

While I dislike bird poo, insect poo, cobwebs and dead wasps I embrace a particularly strong hatred for mould. It's the little spores you see, floating around in the air, getting up my nose, triggering my hay fever. I try to be calm and admire the blue skies above the place where I am sitting, but it's impossible because I'm having a moment. Yes, I'm feeling '**badly done to**'.

The internal dialogue of the '**badly done to**' (BDT) moment goes a bit like this: "So here I am, on my own, inhaling all this filth, and he's off doing his men's ministry thing *makes snarky face*. He's putting those ne'r-do-well prison yoofs before my personal well-being again! It won't do! It just won't do!"

It's a negative thought, and I know for certain that negative thoughts generate negative emotions. And so if I buy into those thoughts, believing them to be factually true, I'm in danger of inadvertently slipping into a bit of a grump. And someone may have to pay for that.

So many marital disputes are centred upon the (perceived or otherwise) unfair division of labour. Whether that is in relation to domestic chores such as housework, gardening, shopping or that more vital, immediate task - childcare.

Conversely much marital harmony is achieved when this division is deemed fair. In my BDT moments, and most women I talk to have experienced them, I feel unsupported and under-valued. And that is when men's ministry can come under direct fire.

I know one mother who would deliberately place the vacuum cleaner on the carpet in the centre of the living room before she left for work each morning. That was it. No note. No instructions. She continued this practice for several years. Each evening when she returned from work she would hope against all hope that the man in her household would have taken the hint and demonstrated his support for her by vacuuming the living room. He never did. She was cheesed off for an entire decade.

I once worked with a mother of three who bounced into the office one morning waving tickets for a trip to Paris. She squealed with delight "Paris! He's got us tickets to Paris for our anniversary! I've always dreamed of going to Paris!" They were a gift from her husband. Her excitement was uncontained. The whole team collectively marvelled at this man's astounding intuition. As we settled down over a brew later that day there was considerable female interrogation. How on God's green earth could a woman possibly get a man to understand that above everything else in the world, she wanted to go to Paris? Her answer: "Every single year for the last twenty years I've asked him 'please will you take me to Paris for our anniversary?' "

Parenting, especially very young children, seems to work well when mums and dads share the responsibility of ensuring that fairness prevails: That no one partner feels unsupported or under-valued by the independent activities of the other. This is the on-going balancing act of parenthood. There is a massive need to be intentional about leading men towards maturity in their faith and becoming responsible fathers. Christian based men's groups can have a healthy part to play in contributing to that transformation.

Hedonistic men's events which centre entirely upon the pleasures of consuming pork-based products, watching sport, pigging out and boozing excessively into the wee small hours may help to get men "out from under the feet" but can that activity bear any lasting fruit in a man's heart?

I'm all for men having fun together but as a wife and mother I would certainly be uncomfortable about my nearest and dearest attending a very rowdy sort of group. We need meetings which encourage our men folk to become better sons, brothers, husbands, fathers and citizens, not ones which encourage them to become selfish, lazy, fat, boozers who roll home under the cover of darkness only to disturb the entire household and vomit loudly on the landing. Those kinds of gatherings have the potential to cause division and tension in the home and may even contribute towards relationship breakdown.

A wise men's group leader will understand that supporting a man with a young family may mean accepting that he is just too busy to attend meetings. However, he may appreciate prayer support, the occasional phone call, being part of a small Whatsapp group or meeting up for coffee now and then.

Meeting up with other Dads can also deliver some remarkable dividends. The UK men's ministry *'Who Let the Dad's Out'* is a Christian organisation which specialises in supporting men with children. They are a growing movement which resources churches to reach out to dads, father figures and their children. They believe that to 'turn the hearts of the fathers to their children and the hearts of the children to their fathers' (Malachi 4:6, NIV 1984) is a powerful way 'to make ready a people prepared for the Lord' (Luke 1:17). They say: "We want to see churches creating spaces where dads, father figures and their children can have fun together, and is founded on the Christian principle of wanting to demonstrate God's love to communities. *Who Let The Dads Out?* provides a number of ideas and resources to 'journey' with dads and their children in the context of family support, ministry and mission."

This initiative creates valuable opportunities for Dads to spend time with their children, in the company of other Dads and children. In addition to this *'Who Let the Dad's Out'* is a men's ministry which indirectly supports Mums; giving them a little guilt free time to themselves, safe in the knowledge that their children are having fun with Dad in a great environment. Everyone wins!

Find them on the web at www.wholetthedadsout.org.uk

A WORD FOR THE MUMS:

Girls, be wary of the BDT moments, they are an early warning signal! So skip the drama and speak up in plain English and directly ask your man when you need something. Do not expect him to guess what your needs are. It is soooo delightfully lovely when the man in your life does indeed 'guess' precisely what your needs are, but it is a rare and magical occurrence which you cannot realistically expect to happen very often, sorry.

Try this exercise: "Please *insert correct man's name here* will you help me with xxxx task, at xxxx time on xxxx day?" Repeat as many times as necessary. You'll be surprised how well that works out.

A WORD FOR THE DADS:

Attend men's groups if you can squeeze them in, yes. BUT, be very intentional about putting the needs of your wife and family first. Plan to spend time with them, listen to them, support them, value them, help them. When it's raining watch films together. Hang out with them. Read stories. Play silly made up nonsense games. When it's sunny go to the park or the beach. Play on the swings, make sand castles. Do your share of the domestic chores.

I believe that one of the key roles of a father is to take care of the mother of his children. Please could you do that? As a mother of four I can tell you that motherhood, from a physical and emotional perspective, is the toughest thing ever. It demands everything a woman has just to keep going. And that woman whom you love, the woman whom you chose to live your life with, she is absolutely right. Your children won't be little for long.

And know this pal; women have long memories; she won't forget that you stood by her and that you loved her, and that you loved her babies, and your future together will be all the brighter for your efforts.

> AND KNOW THIS PAL; WOMEN HAVE LONG MEMORIES; SHE WON'T FORGET THAT YOU STOOD BY HER AND THAT YOU LOVED HER, AND THAT YOU LOVED HER BABIES, AND YOUR FUTURE TOGETHER WILL BE ALL THE BRIGHTER FOR YOUR EFFORTS.

QUESTIONS FOR SMALL GROUP DISCUSSION

DESCRIBE A TIME WHEN YOU FELT VERY 'BADLY DONE TO'.

HOW WOULD YOU DESCRIBE THE DIVISION OF LABOUR IN YOUR HOME?

BASED ON NET RESULTS HOW CLEARLY DO YOU EXPLAIN YOUR NEED FOR HELP AND SUBSEQUENTLY RECEIVE HELP?

IF YOU HAVE CHILDREN HOW HAPPY ARE YOU WITH YOUR PARTNER'S CURRENT LEVEL OF INVOLVEMENT?

HOW WELL DO YOU AND YOUR PARTNER COMMUNICATE WITH EACH OTHER ABOUT DOMESTIC MATTERS?

8. A TISSUE: A TISSUE

Let's take a look at some of the common concerns, challenges and tensions which can arise between **single women**, men in church and the ongoing work of men's ministry.

" HOW COME THE MEN ARE ALWAYS GOING OUT FOR A CURRY TOGETHER?

" HOW COME THE MEN GET TO MEET FOR BREAKFAST?

" WHY CAN'T THE LADIES ATTEND THE CURRY EVENING?

" **WHY CAN'T THE LADIES MEET FOR BREAKFAST?**

" **WHY CAN'T THE LADIES HAVE THEIR OWN CURRY NIGHT?**

 **WHY CAN'T THE LADIES MEET UP TO DO SOMETHING?**

I have seen these questions, and similar ones, posted frequently on social media, as a response to the organising of a church based men's event. I have heard these questions, and similar ones, frequently being asked by women in a private setting. These questions are often being asked by grown up, intelligent, educated, working women. I've heard them being asked by the happily marrieds but more often than not it's the single girls who voice strong objections. I've heard them being asked by women on benefits and by women of substance, by the able and by the disabled. Perhaps most remarkably, I've heard them being asked by women, to women, who are enjoying the exclusive company of women, at a women only event. Seriously. I have.

A senior church pastor, whom I shall call Frank, complained recently that he had his "ears chewed off" by the women in his church when he began organizing meetings and events for men. Frank endured much female complaining in spite of the fact there were already several women only groups in full swing. He was baffled!

One likeable woman, whom I shall call Julie, is an independent professional who runs her own successful business and has an enviable degree of financial security and freedom. Yet she demonstrates foot-stamping outrage when the men from her church meet for curry "Why can't we go out for a curry?!"

"You can, luv, you actually can!" murmurs my internal voice.

There is no apparent reason why Julie cannot go out for a curry with her female church friends. She has a very nice car. She can drive. She has time off work in the evening. She has some disposable income. She has a mobile phone and is well connected with many, many, friends who like her because well, Julie is alright. There is an excellent curry house quite nearby to where she lives. She is extremely fit, well and able. She knows how to eat curry. I can see no viable reason why she can't go out for curry.

Over several years of hearing these sorts of remarks it has become obvious to me that surely there is another deeper question, behind the actual question.

Several years ago I married a man, whom I shall call Bob. Mainly because that's his name. I noticed that Bob would keep a large box of three-ply man size tissues in the top drawer of his bedside table. It was very handy. And yet, as a person who suffers with what I will call year round hay fever, I had not thought of this ingenious idea myself. Upon noticing the handy box of tissues for the first time I experienced several moments of foot-stamping irritation. I actually did. My inner voice demanded to know:

"Why can't I have a box of tissues in the top drawer of my bedside table?"

I wasn't super angry, just mildly irritated, annoyed, a tad jealous maybe. It was as if I had been short changed, slighted. I felt as if I had been purposely left out of the meeting when the tissue buying/locating decisions were made. I was being denied access to something which I really needed on a daily basis. These are not rational thoughts. They are silly, irrational thoughts. I'm fully aware of that.

During that particular season (which soon passed) I was earning more money than I had ever earned in my entire life before. In reality I could have quite easily purchased all the boxes of three-ply man size tissues on the shelf of our local Boots Store, brought them home and constructed my own personal, enormous, ceiling height, tissue box pyramid. I could have. But I didn't. For the next ten years, really, every time I was in the bedroom and needed a tissue I would walk around to Bob's side of the bed and get a tissue from his top drawer.

Every morning, every single morning, when applying my face, I would need a tissue. So half way through the procedure I would get up from where I was seated at my dressing table and walk right across the room, and around to Bob's side of the bed, to get a tissue from the drawer. Pretty soon I forgot there was any other option. I stopped questioning. It became an unthinking habit. I never spoke of this to my new husband. Not ever. Because it would be silly to complain about something as petty as where he keeps the box of tissues, I knew that much was true. On some level I knew it was irrational.

Mornings were pressured. There was no time for in depth self-analysis. I just accepted that is where the tissues were kept. I didn't question it any more, this was my lot in life, I should just be glad I have access to tissues. I accepted that I didn't have control over the supply of tissues. I didn't have a vote over what brand of tissues were in the drawer. The man of the house, my husband, had control of the tissues. I was merely a grateful, voiceless benefactor of the tissue supply.

Until an almost invisible under current of petty low-level resentment coupled with blind unthinking resignation generated a personal epiphany. The question arose again:

"Why can't I have my own box of tissues?"

"You can, luv, you actually can!" murmured my internal voice.

Apparently, apparently . . . there are enough tissues for everyone! I'm not kidding! Just because one person has a box of tissues it doesn't actually mean that the other person is, from that point forward, denied access to their own box of tissues. Who knew? So I went to the shop! I bought my own tissues and put them on my dressing table. Where I could reach them! And now every morning I take a tissue from my own box, on my own dressing table. (A dressing table, incidentally, built for me by my very kind, tissue-sharing husband!) Check out my independent spirit! I'm like some kind of extreme, insane tissue owning adult! Honestly sometimes I despair of myself, with my ridiculous, self-imposed limitations, I despair of my own childishness!

And the good news doesn't end there my friend! ALSO, there is enough curry for everyone! You knew that right? Just because the men go out for curry or breakfast or rugby or pizza or whatever, it doesn't mean that there isn't enough of those things left over for the women. The war is over, supplies are not rationed. If you have a family there may need to be some negotiation over finances and child care, but in reality everyone can have a turn at meeting up and enjoying fellowship with their friends. Holding men's meetings does not necessarily cancel out the opportunity to hold women's meetings.

So with that said, I must now ask, what is the question behind the question? Here is one possibility. I believe that inside each woman there still lives the memory of the little girl whom she once was. This little girl has endured much. She may have made it through the rough and tumble of childhood and teenage years but she still bears the scars of her survival. So often when boys are young they resolve conflict with physicality. When girls are young they resolve conflict by exclusion. That is to say if a girl does not comply with the leader of the group she will be forcibly left out of the game. This operation may have replayed itself several times a day, but in order to function properly, the painful memory of it is long buried. Yet for some women, in the most tender parts of their heart, this unanswered question still persists:

"Why was I left out?"

For some women, who are deeply relational by nature, and long to love and be loved in return, it can be the most crushing of questions. In their darker moments further difficult questions tumble in to dog pile the heart.

"Am I likeable?"

"Am I popular?"

"Do I fit in?"

Exclusion, perceived or otherwise, from some activity may inadvertently awaken this dormant pain and a woman may find herself experiencing an irrational, disproportionate reaction. A self-aware woman may realise on some level that her response just doesn't add up. And then she may feel just plain daft. And here's the danger, her thoughts may then leapfrog from the present reality into her painful past. If she internally regresses to the standpoint of the excluded little girl, she may conclude her hurt is being caused by the men who are leaving her out. She surmises this is wrong! The men have got it wrong! And her ancient, angry questions bubble to the surface with some considerable force.

Unless of course I'm wrong.

And she is right.

And the men *are* wrong.

Which wouldn't be a first.

QUESTIONS FOR SMALL GROUP DISCUSSION

Describe a time when you felt the sting of being deliberately left out.

Describe a time when you felt the sting of being unintentionally left out.

Emotionally was there any difference between these two experiences?

What concerns do you have about the men in your church meeting together without any women being present?

What are your views about other age/gender specific groups meeting together eg mums and toddlers, uniformed organisations, women's groups or youth groups?

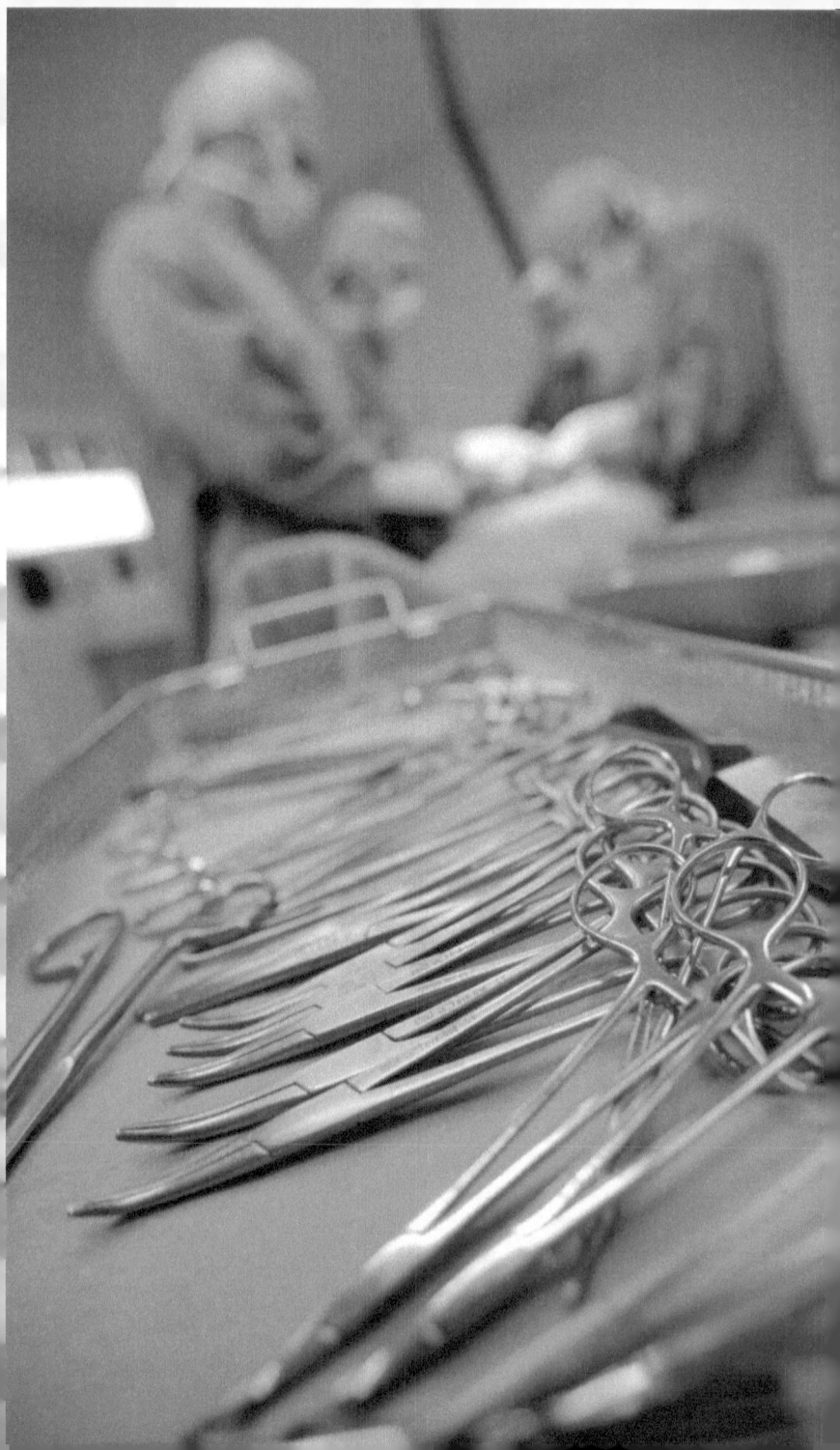

9: STATINS

Let's take a look at some of the common concerns, challenges and tensions which can arise between **health professionals,** men in church and the ongoing work of men's ministry.

" ALL THAT FAT IS CLOGGING UP YOUR ARTERIES.

" YOU REALLY SHOULD OFFER A HEALTHY OPTION.

" DO WE REALLY WANT TO ENCOURAGE MEN TO TASTE WHISKEY? WHAT KIND OF WITNESS IS THAT?

" EXTREME SPORTS COST THE NHS A SMALL FORTUNE IN AVOIDABLE ACCIDENTS!

" SEDENTARY LIFE STYLES ARE KILLING MEN, SHOULDN'T WE BE ENCOURAGING MEN TO GET ACTIVE INSTEAD OF SITTING AROUND PASSIVELY WATCHING SPORT ALL AFTERNOON?

It's not without good reason that some health professionals express concern about the nature of men's ministry. So often, from the outside looking in, men's ministry can seem to be centred around the consumption of high fat foods such as bacon, sausages, bread, stodgy fried foods, pasties, burgers and curries. Sometimes alcohol enters into the equation when beer and whiskey tasting events are organised. In addition to this there can be a strong element of physical inactivity, such as watching spectator sports. None of this bodes well for the sedentary man of advancing years. And let's be honest, that's the case for a lot of men in church.

Over the last three years I've been personally responsible for feeding men with the following: 3,125 rashers of bacon, 2,215 sausages and 1,540 buttered buns to be precise. Add in teas, coffee and doughnuts and the calorific total smashes the million mark. I'm not proud of these statistics. In fact, I'm quite uncomfortable with them.

I lead a team of men who work in the kitchen. Sometimes I'm assisted by a slim man of Jewish heritage and a lean, athletic medical doctor. The man of Jewish heritage cooks the pork. The doctor dishes up the greasy food. I'm a wheat intolerant vegetarian. We're all compromising.

We joke about 'doing no harm', prescribing Statins along with the food and how many men might actually turn up if we substituted fruit and yoghurt on the menu. We remain fully convicted that no man would actually sign up for a healthy breakfast, so we drain off as much grease as we possibly can and consider the bacon sandwich as a monthly treat. We can't nanny these men, they are adults. And so we are where we are.

And then there are all the jokes in men's ministry about not eating fresh fruit. The UK's largest men's ministry organisation is Christian Vision for Men (CVM). Each year, for the last few years, they've put together an annual conference for men called The Gathering. It's billed as taking place somewhere 'in a field near Swindon'. In 2018 over 2000 men attended this lively event which featured worship from Graham Kendrick, a bag pipe player, wrestling matches, Scalextric trials, vehicle displays, tug of war, planes flying overhead and all sorts of daftness. One of the big jokes of the weekend was a brief given by CVM President Carl Beech. Carl is a hilarious natural orator. He decreed that any man who was caught eating fruit at the event would be in big trouble.

Comical photos and video clips of men caught with fruit at the event began to emerge on Social Media platforms. The posts generated significant engagement. Most people seemed to get that this was just a joke, a very silly in-joke. We all know it's a good idea to eat fruit and veg, five a day in fact. But in a politically correct world where virtue signalling is rife, men hardly dare to speak for fear of offending someone about something. They have nothing left to poke fun at but themselves. So how about we just chill our boots and let them have that one?

And then there's health and safety. Again, from the outside looking in, the activities in men's ministry can sometimes seem, well, a bit laddish, verging on the reckless. Silly. Irresponsible. Risky. And some of us don't like risk. It doesn't sit comfortably with us does it? We worry about extreme sports, football, darts, wrestling, shooting, climbing, paintballing, wild camping, making fires, crashing around, horseplay and jumping off things! What if it goes wrong? What if someone actually gets hurt and requires medical assistance? What if you're thrashing around and that 'worst fear of mum's everywhere' thing happens – you lose an eye? It won't be quite so funny then will it?

I'm as paranoid about safety as the next person. Ask around. Much as I would prefer the men folk in my life to sit forever in a soft, comfortable arm chair, in a safe corner of the room, drinking herbal tea and gently reciting poetry I know that for most of them, it just isn't going to happen. I'm not against men drinking tea and reading poetry and I have some lovely writerly friends who love to do just that. But I know that for some men this would be a miserable half-life of an existence. And who wants miserable men folk? Where's the fun in that?

So perhaps now and then we just have to compromise (again) and release men to their boyish 'activities'. Of course we can hope and pray that they'll return home unscathed and exhilarated from the experience. And then we can enjoy having happy men in our lives who are victoriously unscathed and exhilarated.

The Samaritans are a British Charity which began in 1953 in London, founded by a vicar called Chad Varah. He wanted to do something specific to help people in distress who had no one to turn to. The charity offers a telephone support service. They are the only organisation to collate suicide statistics for the UK, England, Wales, Scotland, Northern Ireland and ROI, which they publish in their annual Suicide Statistics Report. It makes for very uncomfortable reading. I found these key trends from the Samaritans Suicide Statistics Report 2017 on their website at www.samaritans.org

In 2015 there were 6,639 suicides in the UK and Republic of Ireland.

6,188 suicides were registered in the UK and 451 in the Republic of Ireland.

The highest suicide rate in the UK was for men aged 40–44.

The highest suicide rate in the Republic of Ireland was for men aged 25–34 (with an almost identical rate for men aged 45–54).

In England and the UK, female suicide rates are at their highest in a decade. Rates have increased in the UK (by 3.8%), England (by 2%), Wales (61.8%) and Northern Ireland (18.5%) since 2014 – however increases in Wales and Northern Ireland may be explained by inconsistencies in the processes for recording suicides in these countries.

Female suicide rates have decreased in Scotland (by 1.4%) and the Republic of Ireland (by 13.1%) since 2014.

Male rates remain consistently higher than female suicide rates across the UK and Republic of Ireland – most notably five times higher in Republic of Ireland and around three times in the UK.

These are heart breaking facts. I cannot begin to imagine the crushing pressure which medical professionals must experience on a regular basis because of this extremely serious issue. Surely any endeavour which aims to give men a network of support, an outlet for fun, fellowship and a safe place to talk can only be a good thing. It's impossible to measure but it may even, in some small way, help to take a teensy weensy bit of pressure off the NHS and Social Services. And men's ministry groups can be a place where our wonderful health professionals can find prayer support and fellowship too.

And here we must not forget the single man and the widower. I have lost count of the number of conversations I've had with these men in the kitchen at our popular 'Breakfast for Blokes' meetings. They seem to gravitate towards the comfort of that particular environment. Some will chat endlessly to me; a busy, befuddled woman wearing a greasy apron. In the main I'm getting on with cooking sausages and only half listening to their woes! My friend says that I'm like a mother figure to them. It's true that some have honestly shared their troubles with me and I have been able to pray over them. But they also benefit massively from time with male friends and opportunities to be in good company.

QUESTIONS FOR SMALL GROUP DISCUSSION

IS THE CHURCH RESPONSIBLE FOR ADVISING ON HEALTH MATTERS? HOW DO YOU SEE IT?

HOW OFTEN DO YOU ENJOY A COOKED BREAKFAST/BRUNCH AT HOME? IS THIS SOMETHING YOU ONLY ENJOY WHILE ON HOLIDAY?

WHAT'S THE MOST DANGEROUS ACTIVITY YOU'VE EVER TAKEN PART IN? HOW DID IT TURN OUT?

HAVE YOU EVER BEEN AFFECTED BY A SPORTING ACCIDENT?

HAVE YOU EVER EXPERIENCED A SEASON WHEN YOU FELT ISOLATED?

HAS SOMEONE IN YOUR FAMILY OR CIRCLE OF FRIENDS BEEN AFFECTED BY MENTAL HEALTH PROBLEMS?

Let's take a look at some of the common concerns, challenges and tensions which can arise between **men**, other men in church and the ongoing work of men's ministry.

> ISN'T IT ALL JUST BASED AROUND SPORTS AND STEREOTYPICAL 'BLOKE-ISH' THINGS? THAT KIND OF THING BORES ME RIGID!

> DOESN'T IT JUST PIGEON HOLE GENDERS IN A WAY THAT'S UNHELPFUL IN TODAY'S WORLD?

> I'M JUST NOT INTO DISCUSSING MY 'FEELINGS' WITH OTHER BLOKES, IT'S ALL TOO SERIOUS FOR ME.

> SHOULDN'T WE BE STUDYING GOD'S WORD INSTEAD OF ALL THIS SILLY BANTER AND JOKING AROUND? IT'S JUST NOT SERIOUS ENOUGH FOR ME.

> MEN NEED TO HEAR THE GOSPEL. WE SHOULD BE PREACHING THE GOSPEL. END OF.

> MEN DON'T WANT TO BE PREACHED AT. WE SHOULD JUST BE SOCIALISING WITH THEM.

> THE MEN IN MY CHURCH AREN'T BOTHERED ABOUT MEN'S MINISTRY. THEY JUST AREN'T BOTHERED ABOUT ANYTHING.

All of the previous comments were made by men who were sharing their views on men's ministry. When I first began my research for this book I never expected to encounter so much opposition from men, to men's ministry. But it's out there. None of these chaps see the point of it and some are actively against it. Most of them had never actually attended a contemporary men's meeting. Some were referring back to an ancient memory from years ago.

These chaps, and many like them, have a myriad of reasons and excuses why they just won't attend a men's meeting. They have made up their minds exactly what it's all about and seem completely closed off to the idea.

Some of the men had distant memories of attending old style gospel meetings. You know the sort, you wear a suit and tie, eat a heavy four course meal and then someone gives their 'testimony' for an age while you sit respectfully upright in a hard chair, trying to stay awake, following a long day's work.

Some men I spoke to had memories of men's breakfasts where the women did all the catering: "Oh yes, we've done all that before, but you won't keep it going."

Issues surrounding which gender takes responsibility for the catering are an absolute chuffin' minefield. You wouldn't believe how many folks, both men and women, feel compelled to share their strongly held beliefs about this matter, without being in possession of any of the facts. Some opinions are quite extreme. It's almost as if the kitchen and by association, the catering, is a 'behind the scenes' thing where outspoken views aren't officially registered. It sits on the perimeter of church life, far away from the main meeting and the ears of leaders, while simultaneously rising up as the primal coal face of tension between the sexes. When a man or woman wears an apron it doesn't half upset some people! True positions on gender equality, egalitarianism, and complimentarianism, very quickly spill out, leaving a bit of a mess on the kitchen floor. These days I'm inclined to go along with the thinking expressed in that popular social media meme; attributed to Brene Brown, it reads: "If you're not in the arena, also getting your ass kicked, I'm not interested in your feedback."

Some of the men I interviewed had attended traditional men's fellowship meetings, sitting through lengthy talks about trains and the like. They can be jolly, friendly places where men gather to socialise without any spiritual content whatsoever. Nothing wrong with that. But one man I talked to resisted joining a contemporary new men's group for six whole months because of his poor experience of men's fellowship meetings. Although he was curious, and despite being invited by a friend every month, he declined because he was certain it would be "as dull as dishwater". He eventually went along. Following the upbeat meeting, with food, live music, breakaway groups, old friends and great fellowship he enthused: "I've never been to anything like this before, it's great!"

We see it again and again. It can take months, and several invitations from a friend for some men to give the meetings a try. Following a breakaway group, where men discussed a particular topic confidentially, there was a very interesting revelation. One lovely old guy said: "I've been going to church for forty years but I've never actually had a conversation with another man about what's really on my mind. Never. It's a good thing to do, we should talk more."

Following a big disappointment which hurt him deeply, another man had essentially left his church, only showing up at Christmas. It took ten separate invitations from an old friend for him to go along to his local men's group. Without gossiping he was able to open up a little bit about the disappointment in a confidential environment and the men prayed for him. He still hasn't returned to regular church attendance but he said: "I feel much closer to God and the painful memory is fading."

Remember the challenge I mentioned earlier about being in it for the long game?

Anyone with responsibility for organising men's events will be very much aware of the challenges regarding communication. In so much as it doesn't always happen! Or at best it can be one way. Not all, but a lot of men are notoriously poor at responding to messages. And it takes much effort and nagging to get them to confirm their attendance at an event. They wait right up to the last minute before committing.

When there's mass catering involved it's essential to know your numbers. It varies quite a lot but average attendance at the breakfasts I cater for is upwards of thirty men from a pool of ninety. Not everyone attends every meeting. The day before the meeting I buy and partially cook a stack of bacon along with a shed load of other things which I then transport to our community room. Typically we will receive at least one text notifying us of someone's attendance right on the wire, but it's too late, the allocated bacon is already being crisped up in the pan! To be fair to those who have 'placed their order' as it were, I need to keep track of the portions. There are always a random number of no-shows and unexpected arrivals. Catering above domestic level is most certainly not my area of expertise. But what I lack in skill I try to make up for in volume. I used to get stressed about running out of food. Lately, I'm less worried by this. After all, they're grown men. I'm not their mother. No one will starve. And there's a bakery just around the corner.

This lack of communication can be very disheartening for men's group leaders who are trying to drum up interest in an event and get organised in advance. And I think it goes some way to explain one of the comments at the start of this chapter; "men just aren't bothered about men's ministry." At face value it can appear as if men aren't interested but perhaps they are just reluctant. Of course there will always be some men who want no part of men's ministry. But for the ones who are struggling without support, bored with church life, feeling friendless, battling with the challenges of life or switched off from God, persistent but gentle invitations, along with prayer, can eventually reap enormous dividends.

It's a wonderful moment when you see a man finally get "switched on". He wakes up as if from sleeping, he comes alive, he's up for all the meetings, he's more plugged into family life, his wife has a twinkle in her eye, he's more engaged in church life and more concerned about his community and his brothers in Christ. It appears to come right out of the blue. But it's often the result of an on-going rescue campaign by a man who has persistently dedicated himself to the lengthy and arduous work of men's ministry. Carrying on when the work seems to bear little fruit is a real test of a man's spiritual endurance but the eventual harvest is a remarkable thing to behold! A wise church leader advised: "Don't concern yourself too much with the ones who really aren't interested, just stay focussed on the ones who are."

Critics of men's ministry are often unaware of the sorts of meetings which can work well. Christian Vision for Men (CVM) Regional Director, England (North West) Bob Fraser outlines the options in his book Beyond the Banter. Bob writes: "CVM currently have a four level strategy for connecting with un-churched blokes. Check out their website for more details but in brief: Level One is about blessing your friends by creating non-churchy events where non-churchy blokes can simply feel included in the banter. Level Two is about blessing your friends by creating social events with a guest speaker who may raise matters which go beyond the banter. Level Three is about blessing your friends (if they're interested) with an exploration of faith where questions can be answered in more depth. Level Four is a bloke friendly church, where men are encouraged to be all that God is calling them to be."

Bob leads his own men's group but also mentors and supports emerging men's group leaders. He shares his insights into the reality of how men connect with each other, he writes: "As I've gathered men of faith I've experienced three shocking realisations. Firstly: We don't talk to each other. Ok, there's some banter, sometimes. But we don't exchange anything that's vital, there's no exchange of meaningful information, we don't discuss our views, our struggles, our defeats or celebrate our victories. I mean not at all, there's a kind of lock down, a no go area, a so far and not any further mentality. Secondly we hardly know each other. Not properly. After our meetings so many men say something along the lines of 'I thought so-and-so had it all together, I didn't know he struggled with depression' or 'I always thought so-and-so was a stuffed shirt, but now I've seen another side to him and he's actually an ok guy.' Thirdly: Partly because of the first two factors there is not as much depth of unity as there might be. These are good, faithful men who are not actively disunited. And yes, there are little pockets of unity here and there. But I think it's fair to say we are more like a collection of individuals than a driving force working together on some great mission.

"The way I see it, there is great value in building a foundation of friendship and unity among men of faith, ahead of the game, off the pitch as it were.

"We are blessed with an abundance of theologians and therapists in the church. Good folk who are willing, trained and equipped to tackle the deepest issues of life. I am not an expert in therapy or theology, my calling is simply to help men quench their thirst for brotherhood."

QUESTIONS FOR SMALL GROUP DISCUSSION

HAVE YOU EVER VOLUNTEERED TO CATER FOR AN EVENT AT YOUR CHURCH?

WHAT'S THE RATIO OF MEN TO WOMEN AT YOUR CHURCH?

HOW RESPONSIVE TO PHONE/TEXT/EMAIL MESSAGES ARE YOU'RE MALE CONTACTS?

WHAT EVIDENCE IS THERE OF MALE UNITY AT YOUR CHURCH?

11: DESPONDENT RESPONDENTS

Just after 8:00am a stranger tapped on the door. He seemed a bit lost and I didn't want to turn him away. Without much thought I invited him into the kitchen for a cup of tea. Danny seemed harmless enough and so I showed him through and offered him a seat.

The band was setting up for rehearsals and I introduced Danny to them. The friendly band leader came over to us, shook hands with Danny and joked about 'not wanting any trouble'. Danny chuckled, sat down, cupped the warm brew in two weathered hands, smiled, and began tapping his tired feet along to the worship music. Danny remained under our roof for almost five hours that day. We gave him a hearty home-cooked breakfast, as much attention and love as we could muster and the genuine acceptance and warm fellowship of 35 blokes. Danny was instantly 'in' with this ready-made band of brothers. He ate, he worshipped, he chatted, he listened to a sensitive and helpful talk from a doctor about men's physical and mental health. He joined in the small group discussions which followed, he met the doctor, he met the vicar, he met young blokes, he met old blokes and everyone else in between. I found out later that Danny had been feeling totally adrift. Having been recently widowed, he was struggling desperately with loneliness and grief.

Also among our number was Jacob, a young widower. Roger was going through an ugly divorce. Frank was unfairly dismissed from his high-profile job. Patrick was battling depression. Ernest had financial difficulties. John was made redundant. Will had serious health problems. A good number of the men had significant heartaches around fatherhood. And a dear, kind priest from a neighbouring parish, who had taken ten funerals a fortnight for the last twenty-six years (including many for young children) was in much need of this micro retreat where nothing was demanded from him.

Every man was going into a battle. Or going through a battle. Or coming out of a battle. Every day they silently carried their burdens, wounds and scars. But on that day they would not be silent. They were knocked down, but not defeated, because on that day they got out of bed on a Saturday morning and made the journey to stand before God to worship, pray and fellowship with their brothers.

Some people feel that men meeting with other men, is absolutely wrong. Some people feel that meeting on a Saturday is wrong. Some people feel that men should get out of bed on a Sunday morning to stand before God. Some men will do that. Some of the time. But some men will not. Some people get very upset about this. Some are anguished or outraged. Some respond angrily.

Some people feel that men should fit into the main church, along with the women and children. Some men will do that. Some of the time. But some men will not. Some people get very upset about this. Some are anguished or outraged. Some respond angrily. Some folks are not shy about making their outrage known publicly.

A post on my public Facebook page, linking to my news article reporting on the rise of men's ministry, triggered a tirade of abusive and hateful comments. All of which are too offensive to publish here. My article merely reported the facts as I had discovered them. It was clear that many of the respondents had not read the article but were objecting to the headline and my continued existence on the planet. Respondents identified themselves as male, female, feminists, Christian, non-Christian, religious and non-religious. Comments quickly escalated out of control as respondents began arguing between themselves. A sort of online verbal brawl broke out on my page. Though I found it very unpleasant and alarming I decided not to let this upset me too much, instead I mentally categorised the hateful comments as mindless 'shouting in public' and eventually blocked 25 individuals.

A public post advertising a men's breakfast event generated the following response from an ordained minister: "Whatever next? Meals for mysogynists? Can't this be a bit more inclusive and not so sexist?" The post appeared in a public Facebook group aimed at supporting the activities of local churches. The group's guidelines clearly state the aim to create a welcoming environment where unsupportive comments of any kind would not be tolerated. In spite of this, nine per cent of the group members endorsed the post with a 'like'. Following a complaint to the group administrator the reverend's comment was not removed, instead the topic was opened up for public debate.

An ordained minister who is a very influential high profile career Christian (currently earning over £100k pa) opened up a figurative can of worms on Twitter when he invited comments about men's ministry. He also requested statistical sources which quantify the efficacy of gender specific evangelism. This generated comments from a large number of his followers, most of whom are also ordained and actively working within the established church. Many respondents shared their views about men's events. The following are just a few comments which are representative of the overall discussion:

"I have no idea on effectiveness, but I don't like it!"

"I think the context is important and some serious reflection should be done about them before starting them or poo-poo-ing them. What is the purpose of them? What are they trying to achieve?"

"I had a bit of a rant about it once and then felt bad as the organisers had been responding to what people wanted."

"Are unthinking stereotypes being upheld at these events and do they promote reductive, often patriarchal views of male/female roles and identities?"

"I find these events decidedly uncomfortable. I'm not sure that pandering to clumsy gender stereotypes is good for the gospel."

"Good for fellowship perhaps, and creating safe spaces. But evangelistically it makes me feel a bit peculiar."

"Lazy gender essentialism. Sometimes vaguely helpful for getting some people in the door but more likely excludes others. Church really should be more imaginative than saying only men eat bacon butties."

"The men's ministry at a neighbouring parish gets more men along than there are male parishioners. Very popular amongst the widowers. I'm told they find it a safe place to talk, which for blokes over a certain age is not easy."

"Depends on your success criteria surely. Reinforcing embedded stereotypes 10/10. Building an inclusive community that reaches across conventional boundaries not so good."

"Our Benefice has these groups. Ideologically I wish we didn't. Practically we end up seeing men once a month, whose wives and partners come to church, but who would never come to any other church event themselves."

"Rather turns me cold to be honest."

"I think the issue with these is not necessarily that they exist but how *little critical thinking has gone into them*. For instance, how much do men's events **reinforce toxic masculinity* (which is totally at odds with a Gospel which requires vulnerability and weakness)?"

*I was interested by the comment (above) from a well-known Christian feminist who is particularly verbal on social media about her experience as a rape survivor. This respondent has posted publicly about her child (who was a direct result of the rape) her own difficulties in forgiving the male perpetrator of said crime, and her aversion to those advocating forgiveness. In fairness to her it needs to be made clear that I, and many others, have great respect for this respondent for her tireless efforts in helping women who are victims of abuse. However, in my estimation she directs a wholly unsubstantiated claim against men's events when she states that: *"little critical thinking has gone into them."* (emphasis mine). I would argue that a great deal of very careful, critical thinking has gone into the events which I've researched.

Furthermore the inference that a Christian, faith-based, public meeting may somehow **reinforce toxic masculinity* is an out-dated idea which uses sensationalist language. *Toxic masculinity* is a term which is often used to describe criminal activities such as bullying, stalking, controlling and manipulating women, also verbal, mental, physical and sexual abuse. The largest men's ministry organisation in the UK, CVM, stands firmly against these evils. Wouldn't any kind of '*toxic*' behaviour, whether masculine, feminine, animal, vegetable or mineral, be utterly at odds with the gospel? And surely, on the strength of that, isn't CVM on the same side as said respondent? Doesn't a ministry which aims to help men be more Godly actually honour the work of feminists?

As is the nature of social media, respondents also posted opinions which are slightly off-topic. Many, however, deemed them to bear some relevance to the original thread. These posts included new discussions about the Mothers' Union and Women's World Day of Prayer. Here are just two of them:

"Having seen first-hand how powerful the Mothers' Union are in Kenya, in terms of practical gospel action, I am reviewing my aversion to gendered events."

"It was interesting that this year's World Day of Prayer was rebranded – they took off 'Women's' at the beginning."

The usual mix of opinion, fact, opinion-presented-as-fact, curiosity, shameless self-promotion, friendly banter and careless quips kept this thread live in the global, public arena of Twitter for quite some time.

Along with the rest of the world I observed with interest as the conversation unfolded. As a journalist I generally view conversations to be a good thing. Even when people are opinionated, or disagree, or aren't in possession of all the facts, conversation is a good way of shaping ideas and working things through. For me, face to face conversation, especially with people I trust and respect, is one of my favourite ways to gather information, learn and better understand.

During my research into men's ministry, I've read many online opinions and witnessed a fair few relevant online conversations. A minority of voices in these conversations seem very angry indeed. Within that minority a few voices are growing ever bolder. Some are using inflammatory language which seems out of all proportion to the subject matter. Comments are verging on the militant, stirring up a camp spirit against the work of men's ministry. In addition to literally reading conversations, I've been intuitively 'reading' the prevailing undercurrent of opinion. As a result of this intuitive 'reading' I knew, somewhere down in my belly, that the day was coming when angry conversations would translate into outright physical protest. It wasn't such a big leap to make because, after all, isn't this how the world works?

I knew it was coming. I'd prayed loudly against it. I banged on and on about it for weeks. I'd warned that if a snake could infiltrate and destroy the perfection of Eden, then how much less could the enemy infiltrate our less than perfect environment? This thought kept tumbling around and around in my head. We should expect it I said. We should pray against it I said. We need not be afraid I said, but we couldn't afford to be naïve I said. I said a lot of things. But when the potentially threatening idea of an actual physical protest reached my eyes, just a few days before Danny knocked on the door, I felt totally caught off guard. Knowing that some vulnerable people would be attending the event my predator detection circuits went into overdrive, rocketing off the charts into manic red alert.

The idea to *"storm a men's breakfast event in protest"* was posted as a public statement on the global platform of Twitter. It came from someone who identified themselves as a retired educator living locally to our meeting. This respondent also identified as female and as a practising Christian. Her comment went live around the time that a gun man had 'stormed' a mosque in New Zealand killing 50 people and wounding countless others. Her post was endorsed with five 'likes' making a total of six people who appeared to agree that *"storming a men's breakfast event in protest"* was a good idea.

This raised a number of very difficult-to-answer questions.

How seriously should threatening ideas which are posted on social media be taken?

Would this woman and five of her supporters actually storm the men's breakfast event?

If they stormed the meeting what would their protest actually consist of? Shouting? Mockery? Throwing eggs? Waving placards? Burning bras?

Should we abort the men's breakfast event?

Should we abort men's ministry altogether?

Should we step up the security measures at the men's breakfast event?

If this woman is thinking of storming a men's breakfast event, how many other people are having the same idea?

Is it legal to 'storm' a church based meeting?

Do we have any protection under the law?

And on a more gritty, less gracious, personal level: Do we need all this chuffin' aggravation on our day off when we're working our socks off to bless others?

Following considerable mental anguish and lengthy prayers the decision was made to honour the men who had booked their places. We nervously went ahead with the meeting as planned and stepped up the security measures. And for Danny's sake, I'm so glad we did. And not just for Danny, but for the women who loved and valued Danny while they were alive and were still able to demonstrate their care for him. I'm glad we held the meeting for the sake of Danny's late wife Marjorie, and for the sake of Danny's late mum Elsie. Wouldn't they be happy that we had looked after their lovely Danny for a little while?

There were other men in our meeting whose mums and wives and sisters have prayed endlessly for them. I know women who have cried out to God, sometimes for years and years on end, for someone to get alongside their beloved son or husband. Rather than accepting the shallow, unsubstantiated claims that men's events are 'lacking critical thinking' or 'promoting toxic masculinity' couldn't it be argued that men's ministry does in fact honour these praying, Christian women?

Whatever way you look at it, that morning Danny exercised his free will and made the choice to walk right across town, seeking us out and knocking on the door just after 8:00am. He didn't knock on the vicarage door, he didn't attend the main church meeting, he didn't even pop into the church's community café which was also open that morning. He attended an event which was specifically targeted at making men feel comfortable and accepted. I thank God that the protestors didn't ruin the meeting. And I thank God that Danny was loved unconditionally and effectively welcomed back into the fold.

QUESTIONS FOR SMALL GROUP DISCUSSION:

ARE EVENTS WHICH ARE TARGETED AT MEN DISCRIMINATING AGAINST WOMEN? ARE THEY SEXIST?

IS IT FAIR FOR WOMEN TO STORM A MEN'S EVENT IN PROTEST?

ARE EVENTS WHICH ARE TARGETED AT WOMEN DISCRIMINATING AGAINST MEN? ARE THEY SEXIST?

IS IT FAIR FOR MEN TO STORM A WOMEN'S EVENT IN PROTEST?

ARE EVENTS WHICH ARE TARGETED AT TODDLERS DISCRIMINATING AGAINST TEENAGERS? IS IT AGEIST?

IS IT FAIR FOR TEENAGERS TO STORM A TODDLERS' EVENT IN PROTEST?

WHAT DO YOU MAKE OF THE SAYING: 'BIRDS OF A FEATHER FLOCK TOGETHER.'

WHAT DO YOU MAKE OF THESE WORDS FROM JESUS?

"LOOK AT THE FIG TREE AND ALL THE TREES WHEN THEY SPROUT LEAVES, YOU CAN SEE FOR YOURSELVES AND KNOW THAT SUMMER IS NEAR. EVEN SO, WHEN YOU SEE THESE THINGS HAPPENING, YOU KNOW THAT THE KINGDOM OF GOD IS NEAR."
LUKE 21:29-31 NIV

SOME FINAL THOUGHTS

All over the UK Christian men's groups are emerging and growing. Christian men's events are more popular and well attended than ever. Men are meeting together to pray, support each other and work to improve their communities. Whatever we think about men's ministry, whether we are for it or against it, all the evidence suggests that it's a movement which is gathering considerable momentum. All over the globe other countries are experiencing a similar phenomenon.

Remember the young tree I mentioned at the start of this book? The farmer's field is pretty wild these days with many species competing for light, yet the tree continues to survive and grow. It's tall and the span of its branches has increased. It now appears to be the home of several creatures, including a sweet little family of Wrens. It's a delight to watch them flit about in the garden.

It seems to me that some works of God start out small and sort of sneak up on you. They can go un-noticed at first. I pray that God might make each of us aware of His hand at work, that we might delight in the blessings of His bounty.

Val Fraser

ALSO FROM VAL FRASER

LIFE IN CARDIGANS is part memoir, part story, part rant. A rich collection of stories each inspired by at least one cardigan. From the beautiful hand-knitted creation gifted from a special auntie to the mass produced synthetic rag worn only for painting and cleaning, these touching and often funny stories, discover worth and meaning in something as ordinary as a cardigan.

THE CASE FOR CARDIGANS is part essay, part story, part rant. Why do women love their cardigans? This insightful essay sets out to explore the benefits of, and science behind, the wearing of cardigans.

THE CARDIGAN DIET This transparent memoir unpacks the author's thoughts about chips, chocolate and cheating.

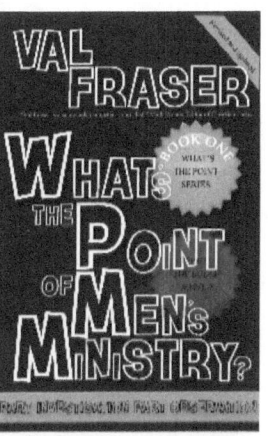

WHAT'S THE POINT OF MEN'S MINISTRY?

This title has been revised and updated and is now available in both hard copy and ebook formats.

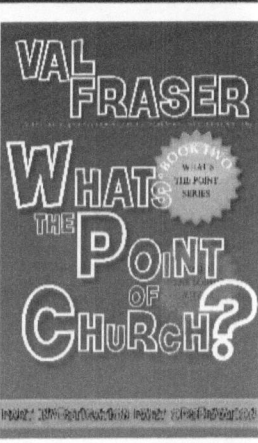

WHAT'S THE POINT OF CHURCH?

This title is currently in development and is due out in 2010.

THE BLESSING DIARIES

Discover the meaning of blessing in this rich collection of musings and meditations. Val Fraser has successfully gathered a creative crowd of gifted free thinkers who see the world with vibrant freshness. Together they have explored and expressed through the timeless art of poetry and story telling, reflection and striking imagery, their deeply personal understanding of the meaning of blessing.

New Life: Reflections for Lent is a collection of creative pieces published by the Association of Christian Writers. Val Fraser is one of the contributors.

BEYOND THE BANTER

Written by Bob Fraser and edited by Val Fraser, this book is a daring discussion about life and faith for blokes. A great resource for individuals and small groups alike. The style and content make it ideal for blokes starting out on a journey of discovery, but it's equally valuable for those who've been on the road for a while and long to get stuck into the meatiness of proper conversations.

ABOUT THE AUTHOR

Val Fraser is a wearer of long cardigans and a writer of short books. She has a working background in journalism and communications and was the Communications Officer for the Diocese of Liverpool before joining UCB as their Creative Writer. She supports the Communications Team at the Diocese of Manchester and regularly reports for Christian Today and other news organisations.

Books from Val: *Life in Cardigans; The Case for Cardigans; The Cardigan Diet; What's The Point of Men's Ministry; Beyond the Banter (editor); The Blessing Diaries (contributor/editor)*. She contributed to New Life: Reflections for Lent published by the Association of Christian Writers.

@ValFraserAuthor   ValFraserAuthor
www.valfraserauthor.com

ABOUT INHOUSEMEDIA

Inhousemedia is an emerging, independent micro-publisher based in the northwest of England. Operationally we function as a non-profit, project-based collective. We specialize in creating original resources which are locally and lovingly produced, sympathetic to the Christian faith and mindful of ethical values.

Our products are available to buy online and at live events. Prices are kept as low as possible - all CDs are a fiver. We regularly raise funds for our favourite charities.

While our books and music CDs have faith elements within them, and are underpinned by a faith in God, we hope they are gentle enough to be valued and enjoyed by those on the fringes of faith communities and beyond.

RESOURCES FROM inhousemedia

The latest Bob Fraser audio CDs are packed with original songs. New releases, audio previews, CDs and digital downloads available at www.bob.frasermusic.com

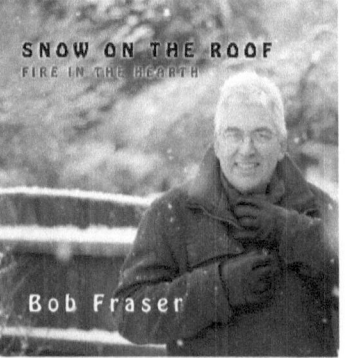

www.ingramcontent.com/pod-product-compliance
Lightning Source LLC
Chambersburg PA
CBHW030441010526
44118CB00011B/738